THE LAW
AND AFTER-HOURS
USE OF SCHOOL FACILITIES

The Law
and After-Hours
Use of School Facilities

WILLIAM J. SMODIC, Ed.D.

M/S PRESS, BOX 5158, PITTSBURGH, PENNSYLVANIA 15206

Library of Congress Catalogue Card Number: 65-23464
Copyright, 1963, 1965, by William J. Smodic
Printed in the United States of America

To my wife Nancy and to our three sons — William Joseph, Daniel Ray, and Robert Allen — for their patience and devotion, their encouragement and understanding, and for their many personal sacrifices.

FOREWORD

INCREASINGLY PUBLIC SCHOOL officials, particularly school board members, superintendents and solicitors, are being concerned with and involved in legal matters. Typically, personnel problems, *i.e.,* tenure cases, have received much attention by writers in the field of school law. But a gap has existed in an aspect of litigation that is important to *all* citizens. All public school people should be especially aware of the issues here involved and the decisions that our courts in the various states have reached.

As public education expands its role and services in our society, we can expect that legal issues will be presented more and more to the courts for solution. This is particularly true, in a new and growing area, of services rendered by the public schools. School buildings are built, paid for, maintained, and used by increasing numbers of people that have not formerly been thought of as students attending the common schools. As our population matures and greater numbers of the older group desire and insist upon services through the public schools, school buildings will be used more and more. And as school officials expand their programs, developing summer services for students who attend during the regular year, as well as opening their facilities to the out-of-school population, it will be necessary for boards of education to understand fully their legal responsibilities in these matters.

It is my feeling that chief school administrators, boards of education, and solicitors especially, must be familiar with details of school law dealing with the community use of school buildings, particularly the permissive aspects of such possible use.

State legislators will also find such information most helpful. I feel certain that these officials and citizens generally do not know of their duties and rights. Dr. Smodic is to be complimented for bringing this material together and making it available. Its pertinence at this particular time is beyond question and its message a necessity to those desiring to render expanded educational programs.

Dr. Maurice J. Thomas
Professor of Education
Chairman, Program in
  Educational Administration
University of Pittsburgh

ACKNOWLEDGMENTS

IN THIS WORK the author has drawn freely upon the writings, surveys, and researches of both practitioners and students of the subject here under consideration, and their great contribution is readily and gratefully acknowledged.

In addition, a host of friends have provided help and encouragement during the writing of this book. It is impossible to name them all, but the author wishes to acknowledge with special gratitude the guidance of Dr. Maurice J. Thomas, whose suggestions and criticism have been invaluable. Thanks, too, should go to Mrs. Loretta McKeating, who offered encouragement, and to my friends, Dr. Clifford A. Burket, Dr. Edwin E. Dunmire, Dr. Joseph E. Ferderbar, and Dr. James S. Porter, whose ideas, coming from men in public school administration, have proved valuable.

Particular acknowledgment should also be afforded the West Publishing Company of St. Paul, Minnesota, for their publications in the field of law, and the University of Pittsburgh Library for making these research tools available.

W.J.S.

CONTENTS

PREFACE

TOO FREQUENTLY ADMINISTRATORS and school board members feel that all they have to do to determine what the law is, is to read the School Code. They do not realize that only a small part of the law is embodied in the Code. Much of it is to be found in the court decisions of the various states. It may truthfully be said that the law is what the courts say it is. The reading of the statute tells us what the legislature has said; but not until the courts have interpreted the law can we be certain that we know what the legislature's enactments mean.

For example, the law says a school board may grant the use of a school building for "any other purposes" or "other educational purposes," but it does not define the scope of the words. To find out what constitutes "any other purposes" or "other educational purposes," the proper source of information is the court decisions rendered in cases where these questions have been raised for judicial interpretation.

Then, too, questions that are not covered by statute frequently arise. After all, the legislature cannot anticipate all the possible situations that are likely to occur. In such cases, one must resort to the courts for answers. They, in turn, search through the law and arrive at their answers in terms of common-law principles.

13

If the statutory language is clear, there is no need for interpretation on the part of the local school board administering it or for evaluation on the part of a judicial body. The terms of the statute cannot be expanded beyond the obvious and self-evident meaning of the language. If a statute is plain and unambiguous, it will not be assumed by a court that the legislature made a mistake or an omission, or used one word where it intended to use another. If the statute covers the whole subject, there is no room for any other rule by implication; the express mention in a statute of one thing implies the exclusion of other things.

It should be mentioned that this book does not purport to make legal experts out of administrative officers or school board members. It is designed only to make them knowledgeable concerning the legal aspects of their jobs, in order that they may thereby avoid some of the legal pitfalls — that they may have an understanding of the legal implications of the various courses of action open to them. To enable the reader better to understand the legal terminology commonly used, a glossary is provided on page 168.

Paraphrasing an old legal maxim, it may be said that an administrator or school board member who, when faced with a legal problem, relies upon his own limited knowledge of the law, "has a fool for a client." Consequently, without some knowledge of how the courts have ruled in questions involving use of school property for non-school purposes, the school official is completely in the dark.

Finally, it is the intention of this book to state the legal principles which have guided courts to their conclusions in interpreting permissive legislation of the several states relative to the use of school property for non-school purposes. All appellate cases involving the discretionary power of the school board are included, together with the specific uses permitted by the school board.

W.J.S.

Connellsville, Pennsylvania
June 1965

THE LAW
AND AFTER-HOURS
USE OF SCHOOL FACILITIES

Chapter One

A LOOK BACK

... AND A LOOK AHEAD

There once was a schoolhouse, a great mental tool house,
  Was shut every night in the year.
'Til the people who hovered around discovered
  That this was a folly too dear.
Said they, "If 'tis ours, then we have the powers
  To use it whenever we will,"
So 'twas opened at night, and to-day with delight
  You can hear them a-shouting their fill.[1]

THE ABOVE STANZA appeared in the pages of *The American Review of Reviews* over a half century ago. And, with each passing year the sentiment expressed has increased in pertinence until it is now almost universal in its application to the public school plant.

For no longer are our schools "for children only." Anyone

---

1. Mary J. Mayer, "Our Public Schools as Social Centers," *The American Review of Reviews,* XLIV (December, 1911), p. 206.

responsible for the planning and/or administration of school plants must be prepared to give serious consideration to the widening use of school facilities by the entire community. Modern America has seen a strong revival of the community function served by the "little red schoolhouse" of pioneer days.

At that time we were primarily an agricultural people, living on farms and in small villages. For protection, subsistence, education, recreation, and numerous other necessities and conveniences, the people found cooperation essential. A well-developed neighborhood spirit was one of the chief results. And from this spirit, as an organized, tangible expression, flowered the community center, with the schoolhouse as the seed.

The school building proved the most practical meeting place because in most cases it was public property. Moreover, its influence was potent and widespread in that every resident made use of it, either as a pupil or as a member of the community. It was non-partisan, non-sectarian and otherwise non-exclusive. In the schoolhouse people of the community met to deliberate upon and to decide matters of government, as well as to attend and to participate in social events. In those days it could truly be said that the schoolhouse was the "Community Capitol."

In time, however, this subsidiary function of the school seems to have deteriorated. Spurred by the rapid growth of urban life in the United States, the school building fell into disuse for community purposes. Concurrently the extended use of school facilities for outside activities was being questioned on the grounds that such use constituted a diversion of public school moneys to private use, and that boards of education had no specific power to grant the use of schools for other than their planned purpose, the formal instruction of children.

One can easily understand how, by the middle of the nineteenth century, a few alert communities would again begin to see the advantages of using the school for other purposes. Indiana in 1859 appears to have been the first state to pass legislation relating to the extended use of public schoolhouses.[2]

---

2. Ward W. Keesecker, "State Laws Permitting Wider Use of School Property," *School Life,* xxx (March, 1938), pp. 3-7, 24.

In 1902 John Dewey stressed four new demands to be made on the schools to meet contemporary needs: social contacts, the development of cultural values and particularly human understanding, training in technical arts and skills, and additional education.

> His was a vision of an expanded concept, in which the school had to undertake an educational function relevant to the contemporary needs of the community, and to "operate as a center of life for all ages and classes." Although his concept could not be realized in practice immediately, it gave great impetus to the movement and provided a sound basis for its future growth.[3]

Since 1900, this limited use of school plants had been of serious concern to educators, civic leaders, and social workers. President Eliot of Harvard University in 1903 said that "There is no such waste of a plant as to shut it up and not use it."[4] And in the same year Sylvester Baxter concurred with this terse statement:

> When the public pays for schools, it pays for institutions in the form of grounds and buildings that be, as a rule, in profitless idleness eighteen hours out of twenty-four. During those eighteen hours they are fenced-in bug-bears, in cities at all events, shunned by the children for whom they have been erected, a waste of investment that private capital would not tolerate for a minute.[5]

The first World War in emphasizing the importance of the community in the development of democratic life, the depression of the early and middle 1930s, and the expanded uses of school buildings during the critical months of World War II, provided the needed emphasis to establish in the minds of the citizenry the importance of non-school use of school property as a factor in the function of public education today. Henceforth the school building could no longer stand apart from the community, with a traditional curriculum and a traditional use. As far as possible the school, through its facilities, should be permitted to contribute to the improvement of living for adults as well as for children.[6]

---

3. John Dewey, "The School as a Social Center," *Journal of Proceedings,* XLI (Washington, D.C.: National Education Association, 1902), pp. 373-383.

4. Sylvester Baxter, "Widening the Use of Public Schoolhouses," *World's Work,* v (March, 1903), p. 3248.

5. *Ibid.,* p. 3247.

6. N. L. Engelhardt and N. L. Engelhardt, Jr., *Planning the Community School* (New York: American Book Company, 1940), p. 171.

Whom should the school serve? Walter D. Cocking has answered:

> It is no longer correct to say that the school should serve only children of certain ages. If the school, as an agency of society, is to justify itself for the period ahead of us, it must be accepted that its fundamental function is to serve the people of the entire community — the very young children, the children of middle years, early adolescent youth, older youth, and the adult as well. It must find a way to serve individuals, the family group, and the entire community. Then and only then, can it be said that the school is serving the entire community, and hence achieving its function.[7]

Yet even today the public school building in America is not being used as widely as might have been anticipated. Constantly ready to serve the adult or general after-school needs of most communities, its full potential has not yet been utilized. Yet there is hardly an activity or field of endeavor that cannot at some time or other make practical use of school facilities.[8]

Through court decisions and revised statutes, the use of public school property for outside purposes has been generally upheld, and wider use of public school property is increasing throughout the United States. As stated before, the basic legal objectives have been two in number, the more important one going back to the fundamental concept that boards of education are agencies of limited powers and their authority does not extend into areas in which the legislature has not expressly permitted them to operate; and the second, more often raised in older cases, being that a non-school use constitutes an expenditure of public tax money for private purposes and is therefore illegal. In this latter connection, the charging of fees to cover expenses or for profit does not reduce the weight of these arguments in the opinion of some courts.

Although the trend is unquestionably toward more liberal use of school property, the statutes and the court decisions of the various states still express widely different views regarding the legality and the advisability of such use. According to one line of local-state court decisions, the use of school property for non-school purposes is prohibited, in the absence of specific statutory permission, no matter

---

7. Walter D. Cocking, "The School — Center of Community Living," *Recreation,* XLIII (August, 1949), p. 253.

8. Robert W. Brittell, "Provisions for Community Use of 350 Recently Constructed School Buildings" (unpublished Master's thesis, Drake University, 1950), p. 10.

what the nature of the use may be. According to another line of thought, which is in the main more recent and which is held by the majority, the use of school property for non-school purposes is permitted, provided it does not interfere with the regular day-school use.

But even within these defined lines, courts across the nation have not been consistent. The same type of statute has been construed differently by various courts. Changing community attitudes and concepts of sound policy, as well as new legislation, have persuaded courts within several states to alter their positions in favor of wider permissible use.

The courts thus are becoming a part of this growing tendency to regard education as something more than mere textbook knowledge and to relate more definitely the work of the school to the life of the community. They realize that school property should be utilized more fully during non-school hours in order to meet the educational, recreational, civic, and social needs of the adults and youth who make up our school districts. And there are strong reasons to believe that the adults are going to use these facilities still more.

> In the past fifty years the average industrial work week has shrunk from fifty-one hours to forty hours, and the rate of shrinkage has been accelerating as the age of automation clicks in. In the next forty years, with developments in solar and atomic powering, many sober statisticians actually expect to see this work week halved.
> Also, as advances in food, drugs and medical techniques extend active life, the great American off-duty group — the children — is being joined now by a new mass, the elderly. Except for churches, there aren't really too many other places but schoolhouses to center their activities in most communities, and as our continent becomes more populous, pressure will increase.[9]

Thus, a new "breed" of American citizen, the elderly, has come into prominence. In the May 20, 1963, edition of the *New York Times*, it was reported editorially that:

> The number of people past their 65th birthday increases by 1,000 every day. The present total of more than 17.5 million is expected to grow to nearly 25 million by 1980. Much more needs doing to assure that the accomplishments of science in extending the life-span will be translated into years of dignity and fulfillment.

Should not the public schools come to represent a familiar and friendly source of stability and assistance to our increasing number of

---

9. Walter McQuade, ed., *Schoolhouse* (New York: Simon and Schuster, 1958), p. 42.

older persons? Who has greater right to their use? As William A.
Yeager has said:

> The public schools belong to the people of a community. These they
> have built and paid for, these they manage . . . it is logical to assume that
> the educational and social uplift of any community should be broadened
> through their use.[10]

Has any board of education the right to say that these people
should not be permitted the use of their own school facilities? If they
want to use their buildings, what reasonable excuse can be made for
refusing them this privilege?

The problem faced by our boards of education is not lack of
money, as is often said, for people are usually ready to vote money
generously for the needs of their own community. It is indifference,
ignorance and an ill-defined responsibility. Those who make frequent
use of school buildings for educational, recreational and cultural
purposes are likely to be quick in their appreciation of their schools
and active in their support.

Education as an institution is no longer in the stage of the one-
room schoolhouse. Large public school buildings are now to be found in
nearly every community, and in most instances they are the most out-
standing structures in the communities. All citizens help to support this
huge public school program, and its activities extend into every home
in one way or another.

The concept of the community school has gained considerable
headway, brought on by the school's expanding use for all types of
community activities. Naturally, problems of operation, maintenance
and personnel, together with costs, will increase. Boards of education
obviously will have to give this matter intensive thought and include
the outcome of their thinking into policies which will be fair not only
to the school administration and the operational personnel, but to the
public at large. For this trend towards greater public use of school
facilities is of significance to all — parents, educators, social agencies
and community groups — in fact, all civic-minded persons. The school
plant comprises a vast and readily available potential which must be
tapped.

The specific uses to which a school facility may be put must be

---

10. William A. Yeager, *Home-School-Community Relations* (Pittsburgh:
University of Pittsburgh Press, 1939), p. 129.

left to the determination of the local board of education. If a particular use of school facilities is not approved by the local board of education, and no state statute exists, there is no general legal action which can force the board to allow the use. On the other hand, there are many judicial decisions relative to the legality of certain uses where permission has been granted by local boards but to which objections have been raised. Opposition has been voiced on grounds as different as the separation of church and state, undesirability of certain groups, or adverse reactions on private business. Thus emerges considerable conflict as to the specific non-school uses to be made of school facilities.

The answer must be a carefully spelled-out policy, formulated after thoughtful consideration of the problems peculiar to a given community, studied in the light of existing legislation, and with an eye towards similar situations which have arisen in other communities. Samples of such policies developed and applied by certain school districts may be found in Chapter Six of this book.

Geographical Distribution of States

New England
Maine
New Hampshire
Vermont
Massachusetts
Connecticut
Rhode Island

Middle Atlantic
New York
New Jersey
Pennsylvania

East North Central
Ohio
Indiana
Illinois
Wisconsin
Michigan

West North Central
Minnesota
Iowa
Missouri
North Dakota
South Dakota
Nebraska
Kansas

South Atlantic
Delaware
Maryland
Virginia
West Virginia
North Carolina
South Carolina
Georgia
Florida

East South Central
Kentucky
Tennessee
Alabama
Mississippi

West South Central
Arkansas
Louisiana
Oklahoma
Texas

Mountain
Montana
Wyoming
Colorado
New Mexico
Idaho
Utah
Arizona
Nevada

Pacific
Washington
Oregon
California
Alaska
Hawaii

Chapter Two

LEGISLATION

AND THE TREND

OF LITIGATION

THE MAIN REASON many people conceive of education as a local rather than as a state function is that the state, in creating the pattern for a public school system, has seen fit to create *local* school districts and to place administrative responsibility in the hands of these districts. However, one must not forget that the authority to create or determine the plan of public education has its origin in the state. The local districts derive all of their powers from the statutes — *i.e.*, the acts passed by the legislature. These districts are local in character and in terms of geography, but they exercise no purely local functions. They act for, and with the approval of, the state. They are creatures of the state, carrying out a purely state function. The state, having created them, is not barred from later doing away with them if, in its wisdom, it sees fit to do so. The state remains free in determining how the schools shall be administered. It may try any plan it wishes, and, having tried one, it is free to change the law and try another. It may retain complete control itself, or it may, as it has, create districts and clothe them with the necessary authority to administer schools. Within the existing school district there is no inherent authority to grant the use of school buildings for non-school purposes. All authority is derived from the statute.

(See opposite page for geographical regions of the United States and the states included therein, referred to in Chapters Two and Three.)

Permissive Legislation

Fifty-four per cent of the states have enacted permissive legislation with relation to the use of school property for non-school purposes. Such legislation denotes a grant of power *to enable but not compel* a school district to do certain things. Table 1 shows the states which fall into this category. It will be seen that every section of the country is represented, the Middle Atlantic, East North Central and West North Central having the largest number of states in this group, while the East South Central has the smallest.

As these laws are examined, it is apparent that the principles involved are much the same, the states in this group having set a definite pattern of thinking in regard to the subject. There is the general feeling that boards of education within the spirit of their power and responsibility have taken the position that our school system was designed to promote public education, and that any use of school property tending to this end may be permitted, provided it does not interfere with the regular school work. These laws recognize the need for placing the disposition of school property for non-school purposes at the discretion of the local school boards; at the same time they urge restraint or caution against acting unreasonably or in an arbitrary or capricious manner.

TABLE 1

STATES FROM EACH GEOGRAPHICAL REGION WITH PERMISSIVE
LEGISLATION PROVIDING FOR THE USE OF SCHOOL PROPERTY FOR
NON-SCHOOL PURPOSES

Geographical Region	Total Number of States in Each Region	States with Permissive Legislation
New England	6	Connecticut New Hampshire
Middle Atlantic	3	New Jersey New York Pennsylvania
East North Central	5	Illinois Michigan Ohio Wisconsin
West North Central	7	Iowa Kansas Minnesota Missouri Nebraska North Dakota
South Atlantic	8	Florida Georgia North Carolina Virginia
East South Central	4	Kentucky
West South Central	4	Arkansas Oklahoma
Mountain	8	Arizona Nevada Utah
Pacific	5	California Oregon

Mandatory Legislation

The legislatures in sixteen states have enacted mandatory legislation in providing for the use of school property for non-school purposes. Table 2 lists these states having laws to which the local school board *must* conform in the letting of school property. This table also shows the relationship of these sixteen states to the total number of states in each of the geographical regions. It can be seen that all but one of the geographical regions of the United States are represented in this grouping of states that have indicated their attitude towards non-school use of school property. Thirty-two per cent of the states fall into this category. No states are included from the Middle Atlantic region, the West North Central region has only one state out of seven listed, while the East North Central has one state out of five. It is interesting to note that of the four states included in the East South Central region, three states have enacted mandatory legislation in providing for community use of school property.

TABLE 2

STATES FROM EACH GEOGRAPHICAL REGION WITH MANDATORY LEGISLATION PROVIDING FOR THE USE OF SCHOOL PROPERTY FOR NON-SCHOOL PURPOSES

Geographical Region	Total Number of States in Each Region	States with Mandatory Legislation
New England	6	Massachusetts Vermont
Middle Atlantic	3	————
East North Central	5	Indiana
West North Central	7	South Dakota
South Atlantic	8	Delaware Maryland West Virginia
East South Central	4	Alabama Mississippi Tennessee
West South Central	4	Texas
Mountain	8	Colorado Idaho Montana
Pacific	5	Hawaii Washington

Silent Laws

Table 3 indicates the states which make no attempt to express the legal standing of the school board in the matter of permitting the use of school property for non-school purposes. Laws of these states have remained silent on this matter, indicating that complete authority lies with the local board. Also shown is the relationship of these seven states to the total number of states within each of the geographical regions. The Middle Atlantic, East North Central, West North Central and East South Central are not included. Fourteen per cent of the states fall into this group.

TABLE 3

STATES FROM EACH GEOGRAPHICAL REGION WHOSE LAWS ARE SILENT ON THE USE OF SCHOOL PROPERTY FOR NON-SCHOOL PURPOSES

Geographical Region	Total Number of States in Each Region	States Whose Laws Are Silent
New England	6	Maine Rhode Island
Middle Atlantic	3	———
East North Central	5	———
West North Central	7	———
South Atlantic	8	South Carolina
East South Central	4	———
West South Central	4	Louisiana
Mountain	8	New Mexico Wyoming
Pacific	5	Alaska

Trends in Discretionary Authority

As we have seen, the law vests school boards with authority and discretion in granting the use of school property for outside purposes. Some local authorities have used broad interpretations in permitting such use. And in some instances, taxpayers have felt that in this discretionary activity the local school board has sometimes exceeded its power, and suit has been brought to stop the activity. There has been a number of such cases from 1900 to 1964.

The appellate court cases summarized here are those which concern the permissive powers of boards of education with relation to the letting of school property for non-school purposes. Authority and discretion were contested with decreasing frequency from 1900 to 1929. During the past three decades, however, the number of litigations has increased sharply. The graph below illustrates this trend. The increasing frequency of court litigation poses many problems to those who are associated with public education when requests for the use of school property are made.

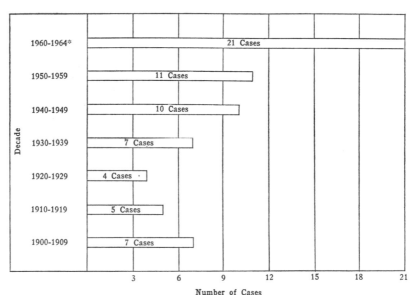

* Five year period.

Court Cases in States with Permissive Legislation

The laws of any state are only as strong as the courts which uphold them. It is important to know that the laws exist, but primarily we are interested in the results of the court cases which have been tried in these states. Greatest court activity is in states where the legislatures have enacted permissive legislation in the matter of granting use of school property for non-school purposes.

Seventy-seven per cent of all the appellate court cases surveyed are from states whose statutes grant permissive powers to boards of education. A total of sixty-five cases was summarized and at least one case located in each of the nine geographical regions. The Middle Atlantic, East North Central and Pacific regions contained the largest number, approximately sixty-two per cent of the total studied. Table 4 shows this number and distribution.

TABLE 4

NUMBER OF APPELLATE CASES FROM EACH GEOGRAPHICAL REGION

Geographical Region	Number Cases Summarized
New England	2
Middle Atlantic	15
East North Central	14
West North Central	9
South Atlantic	5
East South Central	1
West South Central	3
Mountain	5
Pacific	11

The distribution of the sixty-five cases analyzed by date and geographical region appears in Table 5. Thirty-two cases, nearly fifty per cent of all cases (or nearly as many as came to the court from 1900 to 1950), have resulted in the last fifteen years. It should be recalled that the period after World War II and extending into the 1950s was marked by rapid expansion in public education in the United States, particularly at the secondary level, and especially in regard to those aspects of education calling for extensive plant facilities which increasingly reach the population of the community at large. It might also be added that the expansion of secondary education into rural areas was significant.

Table 5 also shows that it was not until the last five years that the East South Central region has had a court case resulting from permissive legislation in this field. The Middle Atlantic region since 1950 has had the greatest court activity. The East North Central shows a slight increase. The East North Central and West North Central have each had at least one court case in every ten-year period, while the East South Central has had one since 1900. With the larger population of our country centered in an area within the Middle Atlantic and East North Central regions and with the recency of educational expansion in the Pacific region, both are reflected in the approximately forty-eight per cent of the cases which arose in these three areas between 1940 and the present time.

The over-all picture, as seen by the total number of appellate cases from all of the several geographical regions, indicates a definite upward trend in the number of court litigations.

A tabulation of cases by states would indicate that in the following four states which have enacted permissive legislation, no appellate court case was revealed on this problem of after-hours use of school facilities: Connecticut, Minnesota, Nevada and Oklahoma.

The foregoing paragraphs suggest that in a broad general sense the pattern of judicial controversies concerning the use of school property for non-school purposes parallels the advance of the expanded concept advocated by John Dewey, that the school must undertake an educational function relevant to the contemporary needs of the community and "operate as a center of life for all ages and classes."

TABLE 5

DISTRIBUTION OF APPELLATE COURT CASES FROM EACH GEOGRAPHICAL REGION, 1900-1964

Ten-Year Periods	New England	Middle Atlantic	East North Central	West North Central	South Atlantic	East South Central	West South Central	Mountain	Pacific	Regional Total
1960-1964*	—	5	4	1	4	1	—	—	6	21
1950-1959	—	6	2	1	1	—	—	1	—	11
1940-1949	—	2	2	1	—	—	—	1	4	10
1930-1939	1	1	1	2	—	—	1	1	—	7
1920-1929	—	1	2	1	—	—	—	—	—	4
1910-1919	—	—	1	1	—	—	1	1	1	5
1900-1909	1	—	2	2	—	—	1	1	—	7
Total	2	15	14	9	5	1	3	5	11	65

* Five-Year Period

Briefly . . .

1. Twenty-seven states — fifty-four per cent — have enacted laws permitting the use of public school property for non-school purposes.

2. Sixteen states — thirty-two per cent — have enacted mandatory legislation in providing for the use of public school property for non-school purposes.

3. Seven states — fourteen per cent — have remained silent in the matter of permitting community use of public school property.

4. States enacting permissive legislation generally permit public school property to be used for civic, recreational, social, and educational purposes.

5. States grouped in the Pacific area generally seem to be most progressive in adopting legislation to permit public school property use by outside organizations.

6. In a great majority of the states it appears that the non-school use must not interfere with the regular public school program and must be subject to such rules and regulations as a local school board may prescribe.

Chapter Three

LEGAL PROVISIONS
AND TYPES OF
CONTROVERSY

EXCEPT AS THE state constitution has limited or controlled the authority of the legislature, that body is free to set up whatever provisions it wishes in determining the use of school buildings for non-school purposes. The legislature's will is expressed through the laws and statutes it enacts. It speaks for the state.

From time to time the legislative bodies of the fifty states have enacted laws providing for the creation, alteration, control and support of a system of public education. These statutes may be thought of as putting flesh on the skeleton of the public school system which was created by the constitution. These law-making bodies are comparatively free to create any type of controls they wish. The laws they have passed define the powers, duties, obligations and responsibilities of the school districts, their officers and their employees. Many of the statutes relate to the use of school buildings for non-school purposes. These legislative enactments are concerned with such things as rules and regulations, authority, responsibility, fees charged and the purposes for which the school board may permit use of buildings outside the regular school program. The powers granted by statutes must be known and understood by every administrator and school board member as they are determinative of their legal rights.

Legal Provisions Indicated in States with Permissive Legislation

Permissive laws providing for the community use of school property exist at the present time in twenty-seven states. These permissive powers of local school authorities as the custodians of school property vary greatly. The school law of Arkansas, for example, states that "the directors of any school district may permit the use of public schoolhouse thereof for social, civic, and recreational purposes, or any other community purpose including any lawful meeting of its citizens." [1] The New Hampshire law reads, "the board may grant use of schoolhouse for writing or singing school, and for religious and other meetings." [2] In Michigan's opinion the local boards may grant the use of school property upon application of any responsible organization or of a group of at least seven citizens of the school district.[3] In Connecticut the school law states that any school district may, by a two-thirds vote of those present at any legal meeting, allow its schoolhouse or schoolhouses to be used for any other purpose, when not in school use.[4] In North Carolina the use of school buildings for community purposes is advocated by state and local officials and it is the custom of the people to regard them as meeting places.[5] The school laws of Pennsylvania and Kansas each contain only one sentence in granting the use of school property for non-school purposes:

> The board of school directors of any district may permit the use of its school grounds and buildings for social, recreation, and other proper purposes, under such rules and regulations as the board may adopt.[6]

> The school board may open the schoolhouse for public purpose, under such rules and regulations as the board shall adopt.[7]

The permissive laws of the twenty-seven states reveal twenty-six

---

1. *Arkansas Statutes Annotated,* Title 80, Section 80-517, 1960, p. 88.
2. *New Hampshire Revised Statutes Annotated,* Title 15, Section 199 :22, 1955, p. 1381.
3. *Michigan's Statutes Annotated,* Title 15, Section 15.3580, 1958, p. 594.
4. *General Statutes of Connecticut,* Title 10, Chapter 170, Section 10-239, 1958, p. 239.
5. *The General Statutes of North Carolina,* Chapter 115, Section 115-133, 1960, pp. 552-553.
6. *Pennsylvania Statutes Annotated,* Table 24, Section 7-775, 1950, pp. 304-305.
7. *General Statutes of Kansas,* Chapter 72, Section 72-1033, 1949, pp. 2216-2217.

specific uses to which school property may be put for community purposes. These are indicated in Table 6 which also shows a geographical distribution (including all fifty states) of these specific uses. States enacting permissive legislation generally permit school property to be used for civic, recreational, social and educational purposes.

States grouped in the Middle Atlantic, West North Central, Mountain and Pacific regions have been more liberal in that their legislation has granted a greater number of specific uses of school property. States in the New England, South Atlantic and East South Central regions have been slow to adopt legislation, and in most instances where they have done so, it is of a general character. The states of the Pacific region seem to be most progressive in adopting legislation to permit the use of school property by outside groups. Of the twenty-six specific uses listed from all twenty-seven states, fifteen are included in legislation enacted by states of the Pacific region.

In general, states enacting permissive legislation have laws which are very elastic with relation to the community use of public school property and as a result subject them to various interpretations and adapt them to local conditions.

Statutes conferring powers upon school boards for the management and control of school property are uniformly worded in general language. The statutes thus are dependent to a considerable extent upon the attitude of the taxpayers and the courts in a specific locality. In a great majority of the states, non-school use must not interfere with the regular school program and is subject to whatever controls, *i.e.,* rules and regulations, a local school board may prescribe (see Table 7). Almost fifty per cent of the states make some provision whereby the "wider use" of schools may be financed by charging a fee, although two states provide this use free of charge.

The Pacific region is the most active in adapting legislation to provide specific controls in the management and control of school property, while states in the West North Central and Mountain regions are next most active. States in the other regions have enacted controls which are of a general nature.

Although the provisions of the state laws are more specific in some states than in others, they have a quality of flexibility which is valuable in that they give scope to local authorities for broader interpretation and thus make possible adaptation to local needs.

TABLE 6

REGIONAL DISTRIBUTION OF SPECIFIC USES OF SCHOOL PROPERTY FOR NON-SCHOOL PURPOSES AS INDICATED IN THE PERMISSIVE LEGISLATION OF TWENTY-SEVEN STATES

Specific Uses	New England	Middle Atlantic	East North Central	West North Central	South Atlantic	East South Central	West South Central	Mountain	Pacific	Total
Agriculture	—	—	—	1	—	—	—	1	1	3
Child Care Center	—	—	—	—	—	—	—	—	1	1
Civic	1	2	2	3	3	1	1	2	1	16
Educational	1	2	2	1	—	1	—	2	1	10
Evening Schools	—	—	—	—	—	—	1	—	—	1
Exams for Selection of Personnel	—	1	—	—	—	—	—	1	—	2
Floriculture	—	1	—	—	—	—	—	—	—	1
Horticulture	—	—	1	—	—	—	—	—	—	1
Instruction of Precinct Workers	—	—	—	—	—	—	1	—	—	1
Lawful Purpose	—	—	—	—	2	—	—	—	—	2
Legal Assemblies	—	—	1	—	—	—	1	1	1	4
Literary	—	—	1	—	—	—	—	—	—	1
Mentally Retarded	1	1	—	1	—	1	1	1	1	7
Political Discussion	—	1	—	1	1	1	1	1	1	7
Private Schools	—	—	1	4	—	—	—	1	1	7
Public Meetings	—	—	4	2	1	1	1	2	1	15
Recreational	—	3	—	1	1	1	1	1	1	3
Registration of Voters	1	2	1	1	—	—	—	1	1	6
Religion — Sunday Schools	—	—	1	1	—	1	1	1	1	3
Scientific	—	—	—	1	—	—	—	—	—	1
Secret Societies	—	—	—	1	1	1	1	1	1	12
Social	—	3	2	2	1	—	—	1	1	3
Subversive Groups Not Allowed	—	3	—	1	2	—	—	—	—	7
Voting Stations	—	—	—	2	2	—	—	—	—	1
Writing or Singing Schools	1	—	—	—	—	—	—	—	—	1
Other Uses	2	1	1	3	2	1	1	1	1	13
Number of Specific Uses in Each Geographical Division	6	11	10	13	6	7	9	12	15	

Maximum number of specific uses in each geographical division could total 26.

TABLE 7

REGIONAL DISTRIBUTION OF SPECIFIC CONTROLS FOR USE OF SCHOOL PROPERTY FOR NON-SCHOOL PURPOSES AS INDICATED IN THE PERMISSIVE LEGISLATION OF TWENTY-SEVEN STATES

Discretionary Powers	New England	Middle Atlantic	East North Central	West North Central	South Atlantic	East South Central	West South Central	Mountain	Pacific	Total
Application of responsible organization or group of at least seven citizens	—	—	2	—	—	—	—	—	—	2
Clause forbidding use by voters	—	—	—	2	—	—	1	—	1	4
Denying use of school building not left as found	—	—	—	—	2	—	—	—	—	2
Determination of intent	—	—	—	—	—	—	—	—	1	1
Equal rights afforded all religious or political parties	—	—	—	1	—	—	—	—	1	2
Extent of grant of use	—	—	—	—	—	—	—	1	1	2
Free of charge	—	—	1	1	—	—	—	—	—	2
May charge fee	—	3	1	4	—	—	2	2	1	13
No cost to district and no furniture removed	—	—	—	1	—	—	—	1	1	3
Not to interfere with regular school program	2	2	1	3	1	—	1	3	1	14
Not monopolized	—	—	—	—	—	—	—	1	1	2
Not for public over the written request of electors of the district	—	—	—	1	—	—	—	—	—	1
Not used for commercial purposes	—	—	—	—	—	—	—	—	—	1
Persons using building liable	1	—	2	—	—	—	—	1	—	3
Rules and regulations	1	2	1	4	4	1	1	2	1	17
Two-thirds vote of school board necessary for use	1	—	—	—	—	—	—	—	—	1
When to use:										
During school term	—	—	—	—	2	—	—	1	—	3
During vacation	—	—	—	—	2	—	—	1	—	3
When not occupied for public school program	1	3	1	—	—	1	1	—	1	8
Number of Specific Controls in Each Geographical Division	5	4	7	8	5	2	5	9	10	

Maximum number of discretionary powers in each geographical division could total 19.

Legal Controversies Resulting from Statute Provisions Peculiar to Certain States

It is the responsibility of the courts to interpret the law. Since it is humanly impossible for any legislature to foresee all of the controversies which may arise relative to a statutory enactment, it then becomes the task of the court to determine, as far as possible, what it deems was the "intention of the legislature" when the law was enacted.

Courts do not act on their own. They assume jurisdiction and dispose only of those controversies which have been initiated by individuals or agencies and referred to them for decision. A lawsuit is started by the filing of a complaint in which certain facts are alleged, these facts being designed to show that some law is being or has been violated.

Frequent controversies have arisen concerning certain types of community use of school facilities. Table 8 classifies sixty-five summarized cases according to date and major subject of controversy. This table also points out the topics which have been prominent in judicial controversy at various times from 1900 to 1964. Group A indicates controversies involving discretionary powers imposed by a school board in allowing the use of school property for community purposes. Group B lists the specific uses over which some controversy resulted. The number of controversies in the last five-year period is greater than that of the preceding twenty-year period.

It would appear that school boards are generally upheld by the courts in the exercise of discretionary powers when imposing restrictions in granting the use of school property for non-school purposes. If a board exercises discretionary power, a court will be likely to uphold an honest decision of the board regardless of how disastrous may have been the consequences.

No significant differences among topics of judicial controversy are indicated under Group A of Table 8. Here it is interesting to note that in the early 1960s there has been increased concern involving the liability of public schools in permitting use of school property by the community.

Special attention should be given to disputes concerning the use of school facilities for public assemblies and for religious purposes since these two areas have been most productive of controversy. This is pointed out in Table 8 under Group B. One-third of the disputes on the use of public school facilities for religious purposes came in the

TOPICS OF MAJOR JUDICIAL CONTROVERSY ACCORDING TO DECADE WHEN CONTROVERSY AROSE

Controversy	1900 1909	1910 1919	1920 1929	1930 1939	1940 1949	1950 1959	1960 1964	Total
Group A *Discretionary Powers*								
Accessory school use as preventing abandonment	—	—	—	1	—	—	4	5
Bookstore operated in public school building	—	1	1	—	—	—	—	2
Legality of school board renting school property	—	—	—	—	—	1	—	1
Public school liability in permitting use of school property	—	—	2	1	1	3	10	17
Public school property not being used for school purposes	—	—	—	—	—	1	—	1
Rental fee for use of public school property	—	—	—	—	—	—	1	1
School board not complying with city ordinance	—	1	—	—	—	—	—	1
School board permitting sale or lease of school property for worthwhile purposes	—	—	—	—	1	—	1	2
School board permitting use of athletic field to group not connected with school	—	—	—	—	—	1	—	1
Total — Group A	0	2	3	2	2	6	16	31
Group B *Specific Uses*								
Fraternal meetings	1	1	—	1	—	—	—	3
Private schools	1	—	—	—	—	2	—	3
Public assemblies	1	1	1	1	3	—	6	13
Public and private dances	1	1	—	1	1	—	—	4
Religious organizations	—	—	—	—	1	—	—	1
Religious purposes	3	—	—	1	2	3	—	9
Theatre run for profit	—	—	—	1	—	—	—	1
Total — Group B	7	3	1	5	7	5	6	34
Total — Both Groups	7	5	4	7	9	11	22	65

period 1900 to 1909, while approximately fifty-six per cent have occurred in the last twenty-one years. The persistence of this dispute regarding the use of public school facilities for religious purposes might possibly indicate that religion and public education are of special concern to our present-day society — and the conviction, prevalent throughout our national history, that the two should remain separate.

The use of public school property for public assemblies has assumed special prominence in the last twenty years, especially in the 1960s. This might be misleading in that the reader may feel that state enactments are prohibiting such usage. To clarify this possible misconception, it must be noted that these controversies have arisen when an individual or group seeking the use of school property is unpopular or has adopted an unpopular cause. An example may be the proposed use of school facilities requested by individuals or groups known to have communistic affiliations. This has occurred in both New York and California.

A distribution of the major judicial controversies into nine geographical regions appears in Table 9. Striking regional differences are shown here. In Group A the West South Central region has had no disputes arise concerning school board infraction of restrictions permitting the use of school facilities for community purposes. Most disputes arose in the Middle Atlantic and East North Central areas.

Group B in Table 9 reveals that the East South Central region had no judicial controversies resulting from community use of school facilities, while the New England and South Atlantic each had one. More disputes arose in the Middle Atlantic and Pacific regions, followed closely by the West North Central. The West North Central also had six topics of major judicial controversy. No other region had more than three topics of major judicial controversy.

The courts are influenced to take into account in their decisions the economic, political, religious, educational and other implications of such cases as come before them. Traditionally, legislative enactments lag behind developments in education. The courts can, by liberal interpretation of the statutes, ease the restrictions of education from legislative controls.

Thus the educational progress in any state will depend to some degree upon the extent to which the courts understand and are sympathetic with the aims and purposes of education.

REGIONAL DISTRIBUTION OF TOPICS OF MAJOR JUDICIAL CONTROVERSIES, 1900 TO 1964

Controversy	New England	Middle Atlantic	East North Central	West North Central	South Atlantic	East South Central	West South Central	Mountain	Pacific	Total
Group A										
Discretionary Powers										
Accessory school use as preventing abandonment	—	—	1	—	3	1	—	—	1	6
Bookstore operated in public school building	—	—	—	—	—	2	—	—	—	2
Legality of school board renting school property	—	—	1	—	—	—	—	—	—	1
Public school liability in permitting use of school property	1	7	5	—	1	—	—	1	1	16
Public school property not being used for school purposes	—	—	1	—	—	—	—	—	—	1
Rental fee for use of public school property	—	—	—	—	—	—	—	—	1	1
School board not complying with city ordinance	—	—	—	—	—	—	—	1	—	1
School board permitting sale or lease of school property for worthwhile purposes	—	—	—	1	—	—	—	1	—	2
School board permitting use of athletic field to group not connected with school	—	—	—	1	—	—	—	—	—	1
Total — Group A	1	7	8	2	4	3	0	3	3	31
Group B										
Specific Uses										
Fraternal meetings	1	1	1	—	—	—	—	—	—	3
Private schools	—	—	—	—	—	—	1	2	—	3
Public assemblies	—	4	—	2	—	—	—	—	7	13
Public and private dances	—	—	—	3	—	—	1	—	—	4
Religious organizations	—	—	—	—	1	—	—	—	—	1
Religious purposes	—	3	3	1	—	—	1	—	1	9
Theatre run for profit	—	—	—	1	—	—	—	—	—	1
Total — Group B	1	8	4	7	1	0	3	2	8	34
Total — Both Groups	2	15	12	9	5	3	3	5	11	65

Briefly . . .

1. More controversies have resulted from school boards granting the use of public school property for community purposes than from litigation involving school board discretionary power.

2. The last twenty years have seen increased litigation involving the liability of public schools in permitting community use.

3. The use of public school property for public assembly has been most productive of controversial topics for court litigation.

Chapter Four

LITIGATION
RESULTING FROM
DISCRETIONARY POWER

LEGISLATION IN THE twenty-seven states studied has kept abreast of the steady demands of citizen groups for more extensive use of public school facilities. As non-school uses of school property increased, so opportunities for challenging the rulings of school boards became more frequent, with the result that court decisions were sought to determine the proper school board discretionary power. Appellate court decisions resulting from actions growing out of rulings number thirty cases which appear to be applicable to basic principles of law.

The legal issues arising out of the discretionary power of school boards in these cases are limited to the following:

1. Accessory school use as preventing abandonment
2. Operation of bookstore in public school building
3. Public school liability in permitting use of school property
4. Public school property not being used for school purposes
5. Legality of school board renting school property
6. Rental fee for use of public school property
7. School board not complying with a city ordinance
8. School board permitting sale or lease of school property for worthwhile purposes (hospital, university, etc.)
9. School board permitting use of athletic field to group not connected with school

1. Accessory School Use as Preventing Abandonment

With population changes, school district reorganization, and other community developments, school authorities may at times find it desirable to modify the use made of certain of their facilities. It is also the responsibility of these authorities to dispose of property no longer needed for school purposes. However, when legal title is retained by the district, there may be limits to the extent to which such property may permanently be diverted from the use for which it was acquired.

In a Wisconsin case,[1] a charge involved the use made of a school building and also which of two agencies governed its control. The City of Manitowoc began action to restrain the board of education from abandoning its third ward school for elementary purposes and, further, to restrain it from turning over said school to the local board of vocational education for vocational training. Except when otherwise provided, the city council had control of city property, but a statute gave school boards power to "select and acquire sites and adopt plans for school buildings." A further statute set up a board of vocational education with power to make use of "Existing school buildings and equipment . . . as far as practicable." The board of education was the agency in control of school property; the board of vocational education concurred in it — thus the use of existing facilities was practicable as provided by statute, and the city council had nothing to do with it. Said the court:

> No doubt the statute presupposes a certain amount of friendly co-operation between the council and the boards, and it is unfortunate that a controversy of this kind involving the welfare and youth of the city should arise; but having arisen, it must be determined in accordance with the law, which clearly removes the power of the care, control, and management of school property from the common council and vests it in the board of education and the vocational board.

It is significant to note that the board of education changed the type of school as the interests of the community warranted.

---

1. *City of Manitowoc* v. *Board of Education of City of Manitowoc*, 201 Wis. 202, 229 N.W. 652 (1930).

A clear showing of abandonment of publicly owned property by public school officials must be made before property will revert back to grantor. A Georgia case[2] illustrates this.

The property in dispute had on it a schoolhouse, a lunch room, and a building used by teachers as a residence. The ejectment action was filed on September 28, 1960. It appeared from the evidence that no classes were held in the school building from the fall term of 1957 through the spring term of 1960. Classes were resumed, however, in September 1960, after another school building in the county had been condemned. In the summer of 1957 the desks and most of the equipment were removed, although some tables and chairs were left, and remained there until the time of the trial. During the summer of 1957 the building was employed for housing used desks and new furniture to be transferred to other school buildings. In the early part of 1957 the Tift County Board of Education had a new roof placed on the school building. Minor repairs were made on the buildings between that time and the summer of 1960, when major repairs were made to place the school building in condition to be used again for classroom purposes. The house on the property was occupied by a Mr. Johnson, a teacher in the schools of the county, from 1957 to September 1960. He was allowed the use of this house by the board of education as a supplement to his salary. For a period from October 2, 1958, to August 1, 1959, Mr. Johnson paid rent to the plaintiff.

It was contended by the plaintiff, however, that a reversion would occur unless the property was used for the formal education of children residing in the territory which formerly comprised the Excelsior School District. It was stipulated that the Excelsior School District was not an independent school district. By the 1946 act (Ga. L. 1946, pp. 206-207) all local school districts in each county, not including independent districts, were merged into one school district, and title to the property formerly owned by the trustees of the local school districts became vested in the county boards of education.

Justice Head, speaking for the court, affirmed:

> Under the language of the deed conveying to a county board of education land "for school purposes" with a reversionary clause as to the title if the land ceased to be used for "educational purposes," the mere facts that the board . . . had permitted a teacher to live in the schoolhouse on the land in question, would not cause a reverter.

2. *A. W. Ingram* v. *W. D. Doss,* 217 Ga. 645, 124 S.E. 2d 87 (1962).

Similarly, claim that title had reverted when school property was leased by a board of education for use as a community center and not for school purposes was immaterial.[3]

The Georgia Coffee County Board of Education asserted that on or about June 1, 1907, George W. Pridgen orally gave a certain tract of land to the trustees of the Pridgen School District. The gift was accepted, a school erected thereon, and the premises enclosed by a fence. The trustees of Pridgen School District operated a public school on the tract from 1907 to 1945 when under the laws of Georgia the school district was abolished. During this period some $24,000 from public funds was spent on the school plant. After 1945 the school was maintained by the defendants until June of 1957 when it was discontinued. During this period the defendants spent $13,000 on the school.

Since 1957 the defendants had leased the tract to Pridgen Community Center, Inc. It was alleged that the defendants and their predecessors in title had been in "exclusive, open, notorious and adverse possession" of the tract for more than fifty years. The defendants requested that the title to the tract be decreed to them.

A verdict was returned in favor of the Coffee County School Board. Justice Almand indicated, if dedication by total silence can arise by implication, the plaintiff would be barred by virtue of the Georgia School Code, Section 85-410, which provides:

> If the owner of lands, either expressly or by his acts, shall dedicate the same to public use, and the same shall be so used for such a length of time that the public accommodation or private rights might be materially affected by an interruption of the enjoyment, he may not afterwards appropriate it to private purposes.

It was undisputed that the Pridgen School Board as well as the Coffee County Board of Education spent several thousand dollars of public funds in improving the property for public use between 1907 and 1957. If the Georgia School Code did not control the issue as indicated above, Judge Almand said the following would:

> If one dedicated land to the public for school purposes, and the dedication was accepted, possession taken, improvements made, capital invested, and the premises used and occupied for such a length of time as that the public accommodation would be affected by an interruption of the enjoyment, then the public (represented by the authorities of the school) would stand in the position of a purchaser for value.

3. *Pridgen* v. *Coffee County Board of Education,* 218 Ga. 326, 127 S.E. 2d 808 (1962).

In the event of a school district's abandonment of a lot of land that reverts to the original owner, all improvements therein shall remain the property of the school district.[4] In North Carolina a school building was erected on a certain lot and a public school conducted therein until about 1951, at which time a new school building was erected at a different location, and no school was conducted in the original building since that date. However, the old building was used by the school board for storing school property until March of 1961 when the school board declared the property to be a liability and authorized its sale, soon thereafter removing from the building all school property and completely abandoning said property for school purposes, pursuant thereto offering it for sale.

The court held and entered judgment to the effect that the reverter clause contained in the deed became operative when the Hamlet City Board of Education ceased to use the property for any school purposes, and that the title thereto reverted to the plaintiffs; that the empty building was the only improvement remaining on the lot; and that the defendant Hamlet City Board of Education should have the right to remove the building from the premises.

An intention of one day using school property for common school purposes did not prevent termination of contract of property conveyed to a school district when a school district, upon abandonment, had failed to use land which was given for such purposes. In a recent case[5] the First District Court of Appeal of California reversed the judgment of the lower court when Palo Alto Unified School District abandoned certain premises for school purposes, and the premises reverted to the grantor's heir.

The parcel of land involved is presently located in the City of Palo Alto and formerly, before consolidation of the two municipalities, in the town of Mayfield. On August 31, 1867, William Paul, as party of the first part, conveyed the land to Joseph N. Spencer, George W. LaPeire and Alexander Young, trustees of the Mayfield School Dis-

4. *Thomas H. Lackey* v. *The Hamlet City Board of Education,* 258 N.C. 460, 128 S.E. 2d 806 (1963).
5. *McDougall* v. *Palo Alto Unified School District,* 28 Cal. Reptr. 37 (1963).

trict, as parties of the second part. Appellants were successors in interest of the grantor. The school board, a political subdivision of the State of California, was the successor in interest of the above trustees. The school district erected a school on the land and continued to operate and maintain it there until 1940 when the building was demolished.

In 1948 Katherine McDougall commenced action against the school district, seeking title to the parcel of land in question. She was largely successful, the court rendering judgment in her favor, determining that she was the owner of an undivided three-fourths interest.

In 1959 the County of Santa Clara commenced the proceedings in eminent domain from which the controversy derived. The three-fourths ownership of the Katherine McDougall claimants having been conceded, the court conducted a preliminary trial of the single issue as to whether appellants or respondent school district had title to the remaining one-fourth interest. After such determination, the remaining issues of the case were tried and resulted in an award of $126,958 in favor of those persons determined to be the owners.

The trial court found and concluded in substance that the school district never abandoned the property for school purposes; that the 1950 judgment in favor of Katherine McDougall and against the school district was not *res judicata* against the latter in these proceedings; that the defendants McDougall had no right or title to the land; and that the school district was the owner of an undivided one-fourth interest in fee simple absolute, and entitled to one-fourth of any award made in the condemnation proceedings.

The appellate court disagreed with this decision. The parties relied on minutes of different meetings of the school board which were received in evidence. The meetings of May 26, 1938, and April 11, 1940, showed in substance the receipt by the board of the district attorney's opinion that the lot in question could not be held unless a school was maintained, and that the tearing down of the Sherman School was considered to involve an abandonment of the site. Appellants relied on these and the subsequent demolition of the building as proof of formal abandonment. The minutes of a later meeting in 1944 indicate that the board reviewed plans for a new Sherman School designed for special pupils. There was testimony that plans prepared in 1945 or 1946 were later discussed by the board "unofficially." Other minutes in 1950, after the conclusion of the Katherine McDougall action, indicated a suggestion of possible use of the site for a warehouse. Respondent relied on the foregoing to negate abandonment.

The court declared that it was not necessary to explore whether the school board did or did not formalize and record an intent to abandon the property. Admittedly no school structure of any kind had been on the property since 1940, and since that date the school district had failed to use the property for any school purposes.

Two separate provisions in the deed operated to bring about abandonment of the property by the school board. First, the deed terminated such estate whenever the school district should abandon the premises. In the court's view, such abandonment was not made unnecessary by an intention to make future use of the property, no such actual use having been made of it for almost twenty years. Second, termination of deed resulted whenever the school district should fail to use said premises for common school purposes.

When a school is no longer maintained, and the property on which it is situated has been offered for sale, a Kentucky court of appeals has ruled[6] that there is clear intention of the grantee to cease using property for its specified purpose, and the board's title is terminated and ownership is reverted.

In 1925, P. G. Hall and his wife sold appellant, Fleming County Board of Education, land located in Flemingsburg adjacent to the public colored school, an area which separated the white from the colored sections of town. The deed of conveyance was similar in form to deeds in general use except for the following:

> It is also expressly agreed as a part of the consideration for the said property that it is not to be sold to anyone, white or colored, for residence purposes and that the said land shall remain a part of The Colored School Property so long as the colored school is maintained where it is now located. In case this part of the consideration is violated, then and upon that contingent the property herein conveyed, together with all improvements thereon (if any), shall immediately revert to the grantors, and the right, title and interest of the grantee shall forthwith determine.

The grantee used the land as a part of the colored school grounds until 1959 when the school system was integrated and the colored chil-

6. *Fleming County Board of Education* v. *Hall*, 380 S.W. 2d 273 (1964).

dren placed in other facilities with white children. Since then the colored school was closed, shut down and abandoned, and neither building nor grounds have been used by anyone since.

On January 10, 1962, Fleming County Fiscal Court voted to sell certain school property including the land in question — the money derived therefrom to be used to retire bonds and to pay interest on bonds secured by the property — and requested the school board to approve the sale of such abandoned property. Thereafter, and pursuant to a resolution of the board of education, the property was advertised to be sold. On the day prior to the date of sale, after first making an unsuccessful attempt to assert their superior claim to the land at a meeting with appellants, appellees filed an action in Fleming Circuit Court asking for a determination of the rights of the parties in and to said real estate.

On June 9 following, the trial court adjudged that the title reverted to grantors and their heirs. The judgment was affirmed by the higher court with the following remark:

> This judgment was based on the finding that the school no longer is maintained, the property has been offered for sale, showing the clear intention of the grantee to cease using the property for the specified purpose.

Briefly . . .

1. When public school facilities are no longer needed for the specific type of school for which they were acquired, the district may ordinarily use them for a different type of school. Requiring existing school buildings to be used as far as practicable for a type of school for which they were not intended imposed the responsibility of the agency having control of school property.

2. The courts have held that land granted for school purposes, with provision for reversion if school use ceases, is not considered abandoned for school use when property is retained for a district park and playground.

2. Operation of Bookstore in Public School Building

It is conceivable that a bookstore intended to meet the needs of a community might be operated in a public school building, provided it is not conducted on a profit basis. This is based on two court cases which occurred in Wisconsin.

In the first case[7] the Milwaukee school board permitted five principals to conduct such stores for the sale of schoolbooks, stationery, and supplies to students for profit. W. D. Tyre, a community dealer in schoolbooks and supplies, brought suit. The principals paid no rent for the space occupied. The school board approved the practice, and the board and the principals looked for authority to a statute which provided that the board "shall adopt at its discretion . . . by laws, rules and regulations . . . for the organization, discipline and management of the public schools under its control and generally adopt such measures as shall promote the good order and public usefulness of said schools." The court held that the statute was intended to authorize rules which were necessary for good order, efficient instruction, and such management of school property as the purpose of public education contemplated. In holding that the school board had no authority to allow a school building to be used for conducting a private business for profit, the court remarked:

> We find nothing in the . . . statute . . . indicating a legislative intent to confer authority on the school boards of this state to permit the schoolhouses within their control to be used for the conduct of private businesses such as the defendants are alleged to be conducting for their personal profit. We think that school boards have not been granted authority to permit school buildings to be devoted to uses other than to school purposes, aside from those uses expressly enumerated in the statutes.

The court indicated that if the facts had shown that the board was furnishing books and supplies as an incident to the efficient conduct of the schools, the result would have been quite different.

This question arose again in another Wisconsin case.[8] W. D. Cook sought to restrain George A. Chamberlain, principal of Riverside High School, from conducting a supply station in a high school

7. *Tyre* v. *Krug,* 159 Wis. 39, 149 N.W. 718, L.R.A. 1915c, 624 (1914).
8. *Cook* v. *Chamberlain,* 199 Wis. 42, 225 N.W. 141 (1929).

building in which books and supplies were sold to students. The supply station was self-sustaining, no part of the expense of conducting it being taken out of money raised by taxation. The board had authority to "adopt such measures as shall promote the good order and public usefulness" of the schools. Plaintiff brought action largely upon *Tyre* v. *Krug,*[9] but the court upheld the practice. The Supreme Court of Wisconsin commented:

> Undeniably the 'good order and public usefulness' of the school is greatly promoted by introducing a system under which each child may, without loss of time, be furnished with the kind and quality of books and supplies (the tools) which are necessary for the prompt and efficient administration of the school work.[10]

Briefly . . .

1. The use of school facilities for operating a bookstore for the benefit of pupils and teachers, and which is intended to meet the needs of a community, is permitted in a public schoolhouse, provided it is not operated on a profit basis.

9. *Tyre* v. *Krug,* 159 Wis. 39, 149 N.W. 718, L.R.A. 1915c, 624 (1914).
10. *Cook* v. *Chamberlain,* 199 Wis. 42, 225 N.W. 141 (1929).

3. Public School Liability in Permitting Use of School Property

School boards often hesitate in permitting non-school use of their buildings since doubt may exist as to their liability should an injury be sustained by a user. Usually the school board in permitting the use of school property for public lectures, concerts, or other educational or social interests, is immune from liability for injuries sustained by a member of the public while on the premises. (See author's comment at bottom of page.) It is contended such use is purely governmental function and is not in conflict with the object for which schools are conducted. On the contrary, such use encourages and advances the interests of pupils and the community, and enhances the efficiency of public schools, even though school authorities furnish utilities and services in connection therewith, and charge a nominal sum to defray the expense.

Thus, in 1927, Mary J. Lincke instituted a suit[11] against the Moline Board of Education to recover damages which she alleged

11. *Lincke* v. *Moline Board of Education*, 245 Ill. App. 459 (1927).

Author's comment: Although not bearing directly on the subject of this volume, the facts concerning *Molitar* v. *Kaneland Community United School District*, 18 Ill. 2d 11, 163 N.E. 2d 89 (1959), should be familiar to anyone related to public school administration. This case has broken precedent exempting school districts from lawsuits resulting from acts of negligence. The Illinois Supreme Court found the common-law doctrine "unsound and unjust under present conditions" in awarding damages against a school district. Minnesota and Wisconsin were quick to follow in similar decisions.

Common law says the state is sovereign and cannot be sued without its consent. Until the Illinois Supreme Court's trend-setting decision, courts had been reluctant to abolish this common-law immunity for schools on the grounds that such a change was the legislature's responsibility. The Illinois decision rejected this line of reasoning in saying:

"The doctrine of school district immunity was created by this court alone. Having found that doctrine to be unsound and unjust under present conditions, we consider that we have not only the power, but the duty to abolish that immunity."

School districts have come under this common-law protection because they are part of the state. Some states reason that districts have no funds to pay damages. Schools are tax-supported, these states argue, and since tax money is not raised explicitly to pay damages, schools cannot, therefore, pay lawsuit judgments.

With school district immunity under common law in a state of flux, and the trend pointing to its eventual abolishment, many school districts now face the question of protecting their financial well-being through liability insurance.

were occasioned when she slipped on the steps of the sidewalk leading from the street to the school building. Her plea for damages stated that the school board had let out the auditorium to a church society for a twenty-five dollar rental; that she paid in advance to the society the admission price for the entertainment; and that the school board was acting in a proprietary capacity for revenue and profit. The Appellate Court of Illinois delivered judgment against her when she appealed to a higher court. The court said:

> It is elementary that the powers and duties of municipal corporations, ..., are of two kinds: 1st, public or governmental, and 2nd, private or proprietary. They are not liable for negligence when exercising governmental functions. When performing proprietary functions they are chargeable with the same duties and obligations as private corporations and ordinary individuals. School districts derive their existence and all their powers from the legislature and have no inherent powers. They have only such powers as are conferred expressly or by necessary implication. School districts are charged with duties purely governmental in character and are agencies of the State, existing for the sole purpose of performing duties in connection with the maintenance of an efficient system of free schools.

In commenting on the rental of an auditorium or classroom, when not otherwise needed, to include the use of light, heat, and attendants, for public lectures, concerts, and other educational and social interests, the court remarked, "the use of school property for such uses is not out of harmony with the object for which schools are conducted, but stimulates and fosters the interest of the pupils and patrons and promotes the efficiency of public schools."

Even though a fee was charged for rental of the school auditorium and a charge of admission was imposed, the school still acted in a governmental function. The court stated:

> It matters not whether the charge of $25 was for the use of the auditorium and a mere incidental charge to reimburse the Board of Education for light, heat, etc., or whether it was purely for profit. If it was the former, we think it was within the power of the Board in connection with its governmental function. If it was for the latter, then it was beyond the power of the School Board. . . . Where governing bodies of municipal corporations engage in unauthorized enterprizes, the corporation cannot be made liable for resulting damages.

Likewise, in New Jersey, John F. Kane brought action[12] against the Board of Education of the Town of Montclair, in Essex County,

---

12. *Kane* v. *Board of Education of Town of Montclair, Essex County,* 20 N.J. Misc. 7, 23 A. 2d 277 (1941).

for injuries sustained as a result of a fall down a flight of steps. He alleged he attended a performance of a theatre group in a school building and that the building premises were under the control of the school board. The Supreme Court of New Jersey, in delivering an opinion in favor of the school board, said, "The Board of Education had express legislative authority to permit the Studio Players, a theatre group, to use the school. The Board of Education did not operate for a profit. There is no statutory authorization for a school district to rent school buildings for a profit." Circuit Judge Joseph G. Walker concluded, "I must reach the conclusion that the statute expressly exempting a school district from liability for personal injuries resulting from the use of public grounds, buildings, or structures, applies."

A school district which voluntarily conducted a summer recreation program open to the general public upon payment of an admission fee satisfied the requirements of a proprietary function and "said school district was subject to liability for the negligence of its employees." In the summer of 1953 the School District of the Township of Mount Lebanon, Pennsylvania, conducted such a recreation program which was open to the general public upon payment of an admission fee. The program, which was not a part of the regular school curriculum, consisted of those activities normal to a summer daycamp, including arts and crafts, dancing and swimming.

A Miss Constance Morris was duly enrolled in this program upon payment by her parents of the weekly charges. On July 30, Miss Morris drowned while playing in the swimming pool. The failure of the school district's employees in charge to give proper supervision, and the rough and disorderly play in the water of the employees and others, were alleged by the girl's father as the basis for court action[13] against the school district for wrongful death. The lower court dismissed the complaint on grounds of governmental immunity.

The higher court had to consider whether the injury-causing activity carried on by the school district in this case was an exercise of proprietary power.

---

13. *Morris* v. *Mt. Lebanon Township School District*, 393 Pa. 633 (1958).

Perhaps there is no issue known to the law which is surrounded by more confusion than the question whether a given municipal operation is governmental or proprietary in nature . . . . In general (and perhaps unhelpfully), it has been said that if a given activity is one which a local government unit is not statutorily required to perform or if it may also be carried on by private enterprise, or if it is used as a means of raising revenue, the function is proprietary.

In holding that there was sufficient evidence to render the school district subject to liability for the negligence of its employees, Justice Cohen remarked:

In the instant case, although the nature of a summer recreation program has not before been judicially determined, the activity satisfies the requirements of a proprietary function. Thus, the school district in this case was not required by statute to undertake the recreation program, nor was the program even a part of the regular school curriculum. On the contrary, it was open to members of the general public residing both within and without the school district. Furthermore, the summer activity was of a type regularly conducted by private enterprises and a charge was made for participation therein.

In another case[14] involving school liability, the question again arose as to whether districts engage in proprietary activity when they permit use of their buildings by non-school groups, especially if a charge is made.

This matter was considered by the Supreme Court of Appeals in Virginia. The district had leased the high school auditorium to an outside agency for a concert. A patron of the concert fell and was injured because the district maintained the floor in a "slick and slippery" condition. It was contended by the injured person that the leasing of the auditorium was a proprietary function. This the court did not agree with, and the district was absolved from the liability. The court quoted the following:

Where those in charge of a public school have authority to permit the school premises to be used for other than strictly school purposes, it has been ruled that a board of education, in permitting a third person or organization to use school premises, when not otherwise needed for school purposes, for public lectures, concerts . . . or other educational or social interests, is engaged in a purely governmental function, since such use is not out of harmony with the object for which schools are conducted . . . even though the school authorities also . . . charge a nominal sum to defray the expense thereof.

14. *Kellman* v. *School Board of City of Norfolk,* 202 Va. 252, 117 S.E. 2d 96 (1960).

The court said that in the determination of whether an act or function is governmental or proprietary the courts have generally applied the test as to whether it tends to promote the cause of education. In the general application of this test the courts have been very liberal. Here the court had no difficulty in determining that leasing the school auditorium for a concert "stimulates and fosters the interest of pupils and the public and promotes the efficiency of the public schools."

Similarly, in 1962, the Appellate Court of Illinois affirmed a lower court's decision when action[15] was brought against the Community Consolidated School District No. 65, the Board of Education, Community Consolidated School District No. 65, and others to recover approximately a half million dollars for injury. Thomas Garrison, while engaged in a dramatic production, sustained serious injuries as the direct result of certain described negligent acts and omissions when a "prop cannon" with appurtenant equipment and flashpowder was ignited and exploded, and "prayed" for judgment in the sum of $465,000, together with interest and costs.

Defendants school district and board of education held that they were authorized agencies of the State of Illinois, created for the exercise of purely governmental functions, and thus immune from liability for negligent acts. The trial court had severed the school district and board of education from the allegations.

Thomas Garrison contended that in presenting these dramatic productions the school district and board of education were acting in a ministerial or proprietary function. Judge Bryant, remarking for the court, said the governmental-proprietary distinction, while applicable to true municipal corporations, had not been applied to school districts or other quasi-municipal corporations which are mere political divisions of the state government. This question was discussed extensively in *Lincke* v. *Moline Board of Education* (see page 55). The lower court decision was affirmed.

15. *Garrison* v. *Community Consolidated School District No. 65,* 34 Ill. App. 2d 322 (1962).

Action against school boards to recover damages for injuries sustained on school grounds after school hours continues to trouble many school districts.

In 1958 the Pennsylvania Supreme Court ruled that P.L. 676. 24 P.S., Section 7-775, indicated a legislative intent that the providing of playgrounds by the school district was to be a governmental and not a proprietary function, and that injuries sustained on school playgrounds by a young boy, as a result of being pushed into an allegedly dangerous fence, could not be recovered.[16]

In a dissenting opinion, Justice Musmanno remarked:

> There is nothing . . . which would suggest that a school district may authorize payment of medical and hospital expenses in some cases and refuse payment in others, once it is established that the injuries complained of resulted from athletic events or games; and if a school district refuses to make payment in a proper case it should be answerable in Court to the aggrieved party.
>
> It is difficult for me to see how much government is involved in a decimating line plunge or in a stampeding intercepted forward pass.

Four years later a New York Supreme Court, Appellate Division, held that the board of education was liable to a boy who, while playing ball in an open playground, was injured in a fall on a patch of ice remaining after recent snowfalls.[17]

Irwin Streickler sustained his injuries in a public playground maintained by the City of New York Board of Education. The accident occurred on a Sunday morning, March 25, 1956, when he was fifteen and one-half years of age. He entered the playground through a gate, kept open in order to allow the public to enter and use the facilities, and was there for the purpose of playing softball with other boys, some of whom were already playing. The ball with which the other boys were playing rolled outside, coming to rest near him and within a few feet of the marked-out diamond of the playing field. As he walked toward the ball, he slipped on a patch of ice. There had been a 13.5 inch snowfall six days before the accident, and another one-inch snowfall the day before the accident.

In the memorandum by the court the statement was made that:

16. *Michael* v. *School District of Lancaster,* 391 Pa. 209, 137 A. 2d 456 (1958).

17. *Streickler* v. *City of New York,* 225 N.Y.S. 2d 602 (1962).

". . . a municipality which extends to its citizens an invitation to enter and use recreational areas owes to those accepting that invitation a duty of reasonable and ordinary care against foreseeable dangers." The danger of ice on the ground may be just as great as that of a defect in the pavement.

The situation here may not be equated with snow and ice on public streets, from which the public may not be excluded merely because of a snowfall; or with snow and ice on private property, from which tenants may not be excluded and from which it may not be feasible or practicable to exclude visitors. A playground can be kept closed until the danger thereon is removed or otherwise disappears. Moreover, while persons walking on public streets or private property may be expected to be watchful for sporadic patches of snow and ice, it should not be expected that young boys playing ball in a playground, or retrieving balls there, will be watchful for such dangerous areas.

Judge Beldock dissented with the following memorandum:

> If this accident took place on private property, there would be no liability. If this accident took place on the public sidewalk, there would be no liability. The majority is of the opinion that there is liability here merely because the defendant Board of Education did not exclude the public from this school yard on the Sunday morning when the accident occurred. I cannot agree with such an extension of the Board's liability. To fasten liability on the Board here would be to impose upon it toward its licensees a duty greater than the duty imposed upon all other property owners toward their licensees.

Judgments delivered in three recent court decisions reveal the school district to be held not liable for injuries sustained on school grounds.

Two cases,[18] consolidated for trial, were brought by Oliver L. Sayers — one in his own right and one as guardian of his son — for expenses and personal injuries suffered by the son, Ollie Lee Sayers, a pupil of School District No. 1, who was injured while playing on the school grounds. The boy suffered injuries as a result of stepping into a hole created by construction work. These actions were brought against the contractors constructing new buildings and against the school district itself.

Defendant school district raised the affirmative defense of governmental immunity. Plaintiff replied, admitting defendant school district

18. *Sayers* v. *School District No. 1*, etc., 114 N.W. 2d 191, 366 Mich. 217 (1962).

was in the exercise of a governmental function but contending that the school district had waived its immunity by purchasing a policy of general liability insurance.

The lower court granted defendant school district's motion for summary judgment, saying the action was barred by the doctrine of governmental immunity and the purchase of insurance did not constitute a waiver of this immunity.

Justice Kavanagh, speaking for the court which affirmed the lower court's decision, remarked:

> We are asked to reverse the trial court by holding the doctrine of governmental immunity is no longer available to a school district. To do so we would have to reverse a number of decisions of our Court dealing with the doctrine of governmental immunity as applied to school districts. Under our decisions the school district as an agency of the State has been clothed with the State's immunity from liability.
> . . .
> The only other question raised on appeal is whether the purchase of a general liability policy of insurance by defendant school district constitutes a waiver of the defense of governmental immunity. It is pointed out by appellant that Illinois . . . has adopted such a rule of law. We find no authority other than the Illinois cases to justify our reversing the Michigan position. We do not feel free to do so in view of the intent of the legislature in re-establishing a defense of governmental immunity in such cases.

Justice Souris, dissenting, said:

> . . . all of the former horror of our common law rule of governmental immunity is restored to full bloom and, by an adroit dribble in this "game of quasi-legal basketball," responsibility therefor is passed to the legislature. What we are told is that the old common law rule of governmental immunity has become a legislative rule, subject to modification only by the legislature, by virtue of simple repeal of a prior statutory waiver of the state's immunity.

The other case[19] occurred in New York. Action was brought by John Bennett, Jr., an infant, to recover damages for personal injuries suffered as a result of his being struck by a stick that forcibly slipped out of a batter's hands during a stickball game in a public school yard, after school hours, while plaintiff was in the yard watching the game. The Board of Education, City of New York, appealed after trial, upon a jury's verdict in favor of John Bennett, Jr., for $35,000.

---

19. *Bennett* v. *Board of Education of City of New York*, 226 N.Y.S. 2d 593, 16 A.D. 2d 651 (1962).

The Supreme Court of New York, Appellate Division, reversed judgment on the law, and the complaint was dismissed. Memorandum by the court stated:

> In our opinion, there was no warrant for submitting this case to the jury. In after-school-hour playgrounds, no duty may be imposed upon defendant to provide supervision over the playground users. Nor may defendant be cast in damages for injuries caused by the act of an intervening third party such as the batter in the stickball game here; the risks of the game were patent and were assumed by the plaintiff as a spectator.

It is to be noted that the attempt by the Board of Education of New York to help children to escape the perils of playing in the street did not burden it with the duty of supervision over the games played in its playgrounds or over the equipment which the participants themselves provided.

If and when a school board permits one of its buildings to be used for non-school purposes, it is the duty of the board of education to use reasonable care to keep the premises and appliances in a safe and suitable condition.

A case[20] in New York is an example. The school board permitted the community center to use the gymnasium and apparatus of a school building during evenings as a recreational center for boys in the neighborhood, with the school principal in charge on such occasions. As one of the activities boys lined up to jump from a springboard over a buck and thereupon to land on a mat. As William Kelly went to the end of the springboard for his jump, two slats proved to be loose and he caught his foot between them, suffering an injury. The boy was not a pupil of the school but was invited as a member of the community to use the building for recreation. He had accepted an invitation to join the group from the physical director of the community center. The board of education was held liable, and Judge Page, speaking for the court, said:

> In my opinion, the board of education is to be held liable in this case upon the following grounds: By permitting the community center to use the gymnasium and apparatus for a community use, there was an invita-

20. *Kelly* v. *Board of Education of City of New York,* 180 N.Y.S. 796, 191 App. Div. 251, Affirmed 180 N.Y.S. 798, 191 App. Div. 254 (1920).

tion to those who availed themselves of the privilege to come upon the premises and use the apparatus. Plaintiff was on the premises as an invitee, and not as a mere licensee. The duty, therefore, rested upon the board of education to use reasonable care to keep the premises and appliances in a safe and suitable condition, so that invitees would not be unnecessarily and unreasonably exposed to danger. It was shown that this springboard had been out of repair for three or four weeks, and that such condition had been reported to the director. The duty of the board was then to remove this defective apparatus and not leave it in the gymnasium, or to take some means of notifying the invitees of its dangerous condition and prohibit its use.

Here it is noted that the injured boy was not on school premises as a pupil or as a trespasser but as one invited to use the recreational facilities. It could be assumed possibly that this same type of liability would extend to any other member of the community who had been invited to participate in an authorized community use of the school's premises.

Similarly, a new trial[21] was ordered by the Supreme Court of New Hampshire when an individual sought remedy of the court to recover for injuries received when he fell into an unguarded passageway leading to a schoolhouse cellar. Hollis, the defendant town, is a single district for school purposes. It leased to the Hollis Lodge of Odd Fellows the third floor of the schoolhouse, retaining control of the rest of the premises. On the night of the meeting, James A. Douglas was injured. The accident occurred after the meeting was over and while the plaintiff was walking towards a parked car in which he expected to ride home.

The court held that since the town had rented the third floor of a school building to a lodge, the town was under obligation to keep the premises reasonably safe for lodge members and, failing this, to be held liable.

Where municipality leased part of schoolhouse as lodge hall, persons entering schoolyard in right of tenant were municipality's invitees to whom it owed duty of exercising reasonable care to have common passageways reasonably safe.

Justice Marble speaking:

. . . That the lease to the lodge in the present case was "incident and

21. *Douglas* v. *Hollis,* 86 N.H. 578, 172 A. 433 (1934).

subordinate to" the general purpose for which the schoolhouse was maintained is reasonably to be inferred from the evidence.

Along these same lines an Arizona case[22] illustrates that school
districts are not free from liability in such occurrences. In this instance,
Edward Sawaya, Jr., attended a football game between Amphitheatre
High School, located in Tucson, and Mesa High School. The game was
played at the stadium of the Tucson High School District. On this
night the Tucson High School District had leased the stadium for the
sum of $300, the rental being paid by the Amphitheatre High School
District. Those admitted to the stadium for the purpose of witnessing
the football game, including the plaintiff, paid an admission fee.

The complaint charged that the Tucson High School District had
negligently allowed the railing on the east grandstand to fall into a
state of disrepair, and that the school district had known of this condition for some time. The plaintiff fell from the grandstand, sustaining
serious and painful personal injuries, and sought remedy of the court
to recover.

In reversing the decision of the lower court, Justice Phelps said
for the court:

> We hold that in leasing the stadium and receiving compensation there-
> for that the school district was in the exercise of a proprietary function
> and that in the exercise thereof it was and is liable for injuries sustained
> as a result of its negligence in the maintenance of said stadium.

In a dissenting opinion Justice Windes remarked:

> A superficial reading of the statute shows clearly that the only pur-
> pose of it is to permit the board to allow, under its discretion and subject
> to such conditions as it may prescribe . . . for recreational, political, eco-
> nomical, artistic, or moral activities. The authorized use is limited to pub-
> lic, educational and cultural purposes. The use permitted here was to
> promote the athletic or educational interests of two other school districts,
> clearly an authorized public use.
>
> . . .
>
> The district board is only carrying out its function as an agency of the
> state in promoting education, the only purpose for which it was organized.
> The fact that a school makes incidental charges for various activities does
> not convert it into a business enterprise.

22. *Sawaya* v. *Tucson High School District No. 1 of Pima County*, 78
Ariz. 389, 281 P. 2d 105 (1955).

In Oregon a school district was held liable when bleachers collapsed, even though the accident had occurred more than seventeen months previous to filing of action. The General Insurance Company, which had issued a three-year blanket public insurance policy to the Gilliam County High School District, claimed the policy was void by reason of the failure of the district to give proper notice of the accident.

The facts in the case[23] are as follows: Effective as of October 9, 1958, for a term of three years, the General Insurance Company issued its blanket public liability insurance policy to the Gilliam County High School District, which insured against liability for claims arising out of damage because of bodily injury and destruction of property in an amount set forth in the policy. Thereafter, Mrs. Denise G. Duus filed an action in the Circuit Court of the State of Oregon for Gilliam County, which alleged that on July 4, 1961, she was attending a baseball game on an athletic field owned by the district in Condon, Oregon, and was injured as a result of the collapse of bleachers on which she was seated. Damages from the school district were sought as a result of alleged injuries received in the collapse.

The policy in question provided, among other things, as follows:

> 6. *Notice of Occurrence, Claim or Suit*: Upon the occurrence of bodily injury, sickness, disease or death, or injury or destruction of property, written notice shall be given by or on behalf of the insured to the company or any of its authorized agents as soon as practicable. Said notice shall contain certain particulars sufficient to identify the insured and also reasonably obtainable information respecting the time, place and circumstances of such occurrence, the name and address of the injured and of any available witnesses . . . .
> III. (a) To defend in his name and behalf any suit against the insured alleging such injury, sickness, disease or destruction and seeking damages on account thereof . . . .

The General Insurance Company contended that the school district, through its agents and employees, knew or should have known of the alleged occurrence involving Mrs. Duus and that it had such knowledge on the date of the accident, or shortly thereafter. The company further contended that the district failed to give written or any notice to its authorized agents, in accordance with the terms of the insurance policy, and did not give such notice until on or about February 12, 1963, more than seventeen months after the occurrence. Thus,

23. *General Insurance Co.* v. *Gilliam County High School District,* 234 F. Supp. 109 (1964).

the General Insurance Company claimed that the policy was void by reason of the school district's failure to give proper notice of the accident.

On the other hand the district contended that it did not have notice of the alleged occurrence, nor should it have known of the injury or the claim of Mrs. Duus, until the time of the filing of the action in the state court, at which time the insurance company was notified. It further contended that the company made and filed a general appearance on behalf of the district and voluntarily entered into and defended the district thus far in said action, and that by reason thereof it had waived its right to claim a defense under the notice clause in the policy.

It was clear that Mr. Brown, the principal of Gilliam County High School, and Mr. Wilson, one of the school board members, were present at the time the bleachers collapsed. At the time, Mr. Wilson noticed the bleachers move sidewise and slowly settle to the ground. He then investigated and did not find anyone that was injured. Mr. Brown also investigated to see if anyone was trapped in the bleachers. He heard that a woman had been taken aside, but he felt there was no injury of any consequence. Mr. Chambers, the school property custodian, who was present, also said that he observed no one who was injured in the collapse. Mr. Brown reported the incident at the next school board meeting, which was probably in July or in August, and told Mr. Pattee, chairman of the board, that someone went to a Dr. Thomas' office after the collapse, but that the doctor had advised that no one was hurt. The other school board members testified that the collapse of the bleachers was discussed at the next school board meeting, but that it was reported to them by the principal that there were no injuries. There is evidence that Mrs. Duus was surrounded by a group of people shortly after the collapse and that she was taken from the field to the doctor's office, where he gave her a "shot" and dismissed her. She was not carried from the field.

The overwhelming weight of evidence supported the view that the school district neither knew, nor had reasonable grounds to believe, that Mrs. Duus received injuries of any consequence on the collapse of the bleachers.

Although the policy was positive in its language requiring the insured to give notice immediately after an accident, such a provision had been construed to mean that the insured must give notice on becoming apprised of the occurrence or at such time that sufficient information was received to place a reasonable person on notice of the fact that there had been an occurrence within the meaning of the policy. Where the information as to the happening of an accident is indefinite and uncertain, the question of whether such information constitutes notice of an assured that an accident has occurred is a question of fact, rather than a question of law. Delay in giving notice is excusable in case of an occurrence which seems to be trivial and results in no apparent harm, or which furnishes no grounds for the insured, acting as a reasonable and prudent person, to believe at the time that a claim for damage will arise.

Otherwise stated, it is not every mishap or occurrence that the assured, under such a policy of liability insurance, must regard as an accident of which immediate notice should be given to the insurance company, even though hindsight, rather than foresight, may discover an injury of a serious nature.

Thus, the school district here was held liable and the General Insurance Company had to pay for injuries only to the extent of the coverage of the policy. It is interesting to note that beyond that, the sovereign immunity of the school district would intervene.

In an Illinois suit[24] a football game patron injured in an accident somewhat similar to *Sawaya* v. *Tucson High School District* (see page 65) could not collect.

The plaintiff, Henry Ludwig, charged in an amended complaint that on October 4, 1956, he purchased a ticket to a football game between two high schools of the City of Chicago and that due to the negligence of the defendant, the board of education, he was injured when he fell on the stairs of the football stadium, which was in the possession and under the control of the defendant.

The question was whether a school board is liable for damages under the facts and circumstances alleged in the amended complaint. The plaintiff emphasized that he was a paying patron at a game presented for profit, and he argued that running a football game for profit is a private and proprietary undertaking not related to any educational

24. *Ludwig* v. *Board of Education*, 35 Ill. App. 2d 401, 183 N.E. 2d 32 (1962).

or governmental function of the defendant school district's program.

In affirming a lower court's decision Justice Dempsey noted:

> The difference between proprietary and governmental functions is of importance in determining the liability of municipal corporations for the tortious conduct of their officers, agents and employees. In Illinois a distinction is made between voluntary municipal corporations such as cities, towns and incorporated villages and involuntary, quasi-municipal corporations such as school districts, boards of education, counties and park districts, which have been created as divisions of the State to aid in the general administration of the State government. The former have been held not subject to liability for torts occurring in the performance of governmental functions but liable for those arising from proprietary functions, while the latter, in the absence of a statute imposing liability, have been held immune from all tort liability.

Boards of education must be constantly aware of the liability imposed when permitting school facilities to be used by outsiders. A recent New York trial court decision was reversed[25] when it was revealed that a school board was held liable for injury to an individual attending graduation exercises.

The injured, Miss Doris Murphy, left the premises of the John F. Hughes School after such exercises, leaving the gymnasium in the building with friends about 9:45 in the evening, going out by a door different from the one by which she had entered, and climbed the stairs with one of her friends. Two others climbed a macadam-paved road on a ramp which was alongside the stairs. At the head of the stairs was a concrete sidewalk which turned toward the ramp and a public street. After taking five or six steps on the walk toward the street, she stepped off upon the ramp some six or seven inches lower and was injured when she fell down onto the ramp. There was a light located at the head of the stairs which would have shed light upon the walk and stairs. The light was part of the original structure, but it was without a bulb.

On direct examination Miss Murphy indicated she had turned at an angle on "what she thought was a flat surface" and as she stepped, she stepped into space and fell. She was invited to use the walk and the area which should have been adequately lighted. The proof submitted showed the existence of electric light fixtures at the head of the stairs.

---

25. *Murphy* v. *Board of Education of the City of Utica,* 244 N.Y.S. 2d 986 (1964).

Error of judgment alone does not carry liability with it, for error of judgment alone is consistent with reasonable care. But failure to abate dangers which reasonable care would have revealed would be cause for liability in this case whether the form of action be negligence or nuisance. The unguarded drop-off from the sidewalk to the ramp might well be found to constitute an inherently dangerous condition in this case which cast upon the school board a duty to illuminate the area where the accident occurred.

In reversing the lower court's decision, the court record relates:

> But the duty to keep the light in repair and functioning was ministerial and the failure or neglect in keeping it lighted is ministerial and for neglect to perform such a duty an action may lie at the behest of the person injured, if defendant had actual or constructive notice of the failure of the light to function. There was not proof of actual notice. The only proof of constructive notice is that the light was defective for lack of a bulb. It might have been found from the established facts that the light fixture was above the reach of persons standing on the ground, that there was no light bulb in it at the time of the accident, and that photographs taken the following day show that there was no bulb in it then. While concededly the proof of constructive notice in this case was very slight, we believe that in the interests of justice, the plaintiff should have an opportunity to present such additional proof as she may have upon this subject. The plaintiff was justified in accepting the invitation to use the walk as she did, but it may be that by lack of illumination she stepped into this unobserved depression with the resulting injuries. Whether or not it should have been seen is clearly a question of fact, but not of law. Lack of illumination may have prevented the appellant from observing this difference in elevations.

Briefly . . .

1. The school board is usually immune from liability for injuries sustained by a member of the public while on school premises, when use of school property not otherwise needed for school purposes is permitted, and when such uses are not out of harmony with the object for which schools are conducted but, instead, stimulate and foster the interest of pupils and patrons and promote the efficiency of the school. Even though a fee may be charged for rental of the property and an admission fee charged, a school still could act in a governmental fashion.

2. Charging for profit by a board of education to part of public using schoolrooms for social purposes is ultra vires.

3. A school district leasing school property and receiving compensation therefor could be in the exercise of a proprietary function and in the exercise thereof is liable for injuries sustained as a result of negligence.

4. By permitting the use of school property for community purposes, there is an invitation to those who avail themselves of the privileges to come upon the premises and use the facilities. Thus, the school district is held liable if reasonable care is not used to keep the premises in a safe and suitable condition, so that invitees would not be unnecessarily and unreasonably exposed to danger.

4. Public School Property Not Being Used for School Purposes

After land has been conveyed for public school purposes, question arises as to whether a school district has claim to property when it ceases to use such property for the purpose intended.

Thus in 1950 Charles H. Koonz brought action[26] against Joint School District No. 4, Village of Gresham, Shawano County, Wisconsin, to enforce a clause in a deed which provided for reversion of land conveyed to a school district in the event the district ceased to use the land for school purposes. A school was maintained on the lot until 1943, when the district transported the children to a school six miles away. From 1943 to 1948, the school district retained its building intact with all equipment, books and a coal supply in readiness for use. The board held annual meetings in the building and kept up the insurance. Charles H. Koonz signed statements he would not attempt to claim the land through reversion. However, when the school board advertised the building for sale in 1948, and passed a motion that the property be retained for a district park and playground, the plaintiff claimed the property had been abandoned and thus reverted to him. The court refused to uphold the claim. It stated:

> The action of the school board herein dedicating the land for park and playground purposes and ordering trees to be planted before a forfeiture was claimed, showed an intention to continue to use the property for school purposes. This definite action substantiates the school board's claim that there was no abandonment and none was contemplated.

The court noted that during the war emergency leniency should be allowed regarding compliance with the conditions of this case.

Briefly . . .

1. The courts have held that land granted for school purposes, with provision for reversion if school use ceases, is not abandoned for school use when property is retained for a district park and playground.

26. *Koonz* v. *Joint School District No. 4, Valley of Gresham, Shawano County,* 256 Wis. 456, 41 N.W. 2d 616 (1950).

5. Legality of School Board Renting School Property

Courts are not in agreement on the extent to which school property may be rented by a school board to others for strictly commercial purposes. A case[27] in this area was decided by the Court of Appeals of Ohio. Here the Struthers City Board of Education and its members entered into an agreement whereby the fieldhouse had been rented to John Scott "for the purpose of holding sporting events," and unless such use was enjoined, such unlawful use should continue in violation of the lawful use for which the building was constructed and might be used, contrary to the intent of the taxpayers and electors of Struthers School District.

The effect of the board's reply was that it had the right to enter into such an agreement for the use of the fieldhouse. The higher court held that the taxpayer who brought this action to enjoin the board from carrying out this contract had the right to attempt to prove that the contract was made to an individual and not to "any responsible organization, or a group of at least seven citizens," as the statute permits. The Ohio Court of Appeals reversed the judgment of the trial court by stating that the Court of Common Pleas erred, and the case was ordered back to the trial court for further proceedings according to law.

Briefly . . .

1. A group of at least seven citizens must make application for the use of school property for non-school purposes.

27. *Serich* v. *Struthers City Board of Education*, 74 Abs. 22, 140 N.E. 2d 31 (Ohio App. 1955).

6. Rental Fee for Use of Public School Property

It is clear that if a board of education charges a rental rate in excess of an amount sufficient to pay the district's cost of supplies, utilities, and salaries necessitated by use of school property, the board is exceeding its legislative power. In a California case[28] in 1960, the Henry George School of Social Science of San Diego brought action to prevent the Governing Board of the San Diego Unified School District from enforcing a rental scheduled in alleged excess of the amount permitted by statute. Rental fees had been changed from $3.50 per two-hour meeting to $7.00 per two-hour classroom meeting, with $1.25 for each additional room over one and $2.50 for each additional hour over two. The trial court dismissed the complaint and the Henry George School of Social Science appealed to the District Court of Appeals. Speaking for the court, Judge Shepard noted:

> It is clear that if the Board is charging a rate greater than or which exceeds "an amount sufficient to pay the cost to the district of supplies, utilities, and salaries paid school district employees necessitated by such use of schoolhouses, property, and grounds of the district 'the governing board' is *exceeding its legislative powers.*" The statute is controlling, and regulations or terms and conditions made by the board in conflict therewith are invalid. Thus it is clear that if the governing board does exceed its jurisdiction the courts will, in proper case, intervene. There is no question that the board's power to fix a rate *within the limitation* fixed by the statute is entirely within the discretionary power of the board, and when such limitation is not exceeded no court will ordinarily interfere in any way with the board's action.

Thus, the District Court of Appeals, Fourth District of California, reversed the earlier decision and reverted the matter back to the San Diego Unified School District Governing Board for further proceedings.

Briefly . . .

1. A school board exceeds its legislative power when it is clear that it charges a rental rate greater than or in excess of an amount sufficient to pay the cost to a school district of supplies, utilities, and salaries paid school employees necessitated by the use of school property for non-school purposes.

28. *Henry George School of Social Science* v. *San Diego Unified School District,* 183 Cal. 2d 82, 6 Cal. Reptr. 661 (1960).

7. School Board Not Complying with a City Ordinance

Sometimes conflicts come before the court which involve the exercise of police power both by the municipality and by the school board. Concerning this matter, a Utah case[29] is in point. Salt Lake City commenced action to enjoin the Board of Education of Salt Lake City "from proceeding further in the construction" of a certain school building until the ordinances should have been complied with. It stated that the Board of Education of Salt Lake City made and entered into a contract for the erection of a three-story, nine-room annex to the summer school building in Salt Lake City, Utah, with full knowledge that the specifications for the annex were not in conformity with the building code. The statutes did not specifically authorize the city to exercise police power with respect to school buildings. The lower court ruled in favor of Salt Lake City, but the Supreme Court of Utah reversed the decision on grounds that the control of and the use permitted of school property were not conferred upon city authorities. The court stated:

> In framing the school laws, in fixing the limitations respecting taxation, in conferring powers on city authorities as well as on the boards of education in cities, the Legislature had all these matters in mind, thence did not intend to confer unnecessary powers on the city authorities respecting the control of public school buildings and did not intend to hamper the school boards in the control of such buildings. . . .
> The fact that the law provides for nonpartisan boards of education; that the members usually are men of experience and are first-class citizens, and thus are not only well qualified to provide for the construction and use of school buildings, but are also competent to safeguard the welfare of the school children as well as that of the public — all convinces the disinterested mind that it was not intended to have a divided control of our public school buildings.

Briefly . . .

1. The control of and the use permitted of school property are not conferred upon city authorities but upon the board of education.

---

29. *Salt Lake City* v. *Board of Education of Salt Lake City,* 52 Utah 540, 175 P. 654 (1918).

8. School Board Permitting Sale or Lease of School Property for Worthwhile Purposes (Hospital, University, etc.)

Occasionally a school district may own property which is not needed for school purposes, and the question arises as to whether the property may be leased for non-school uses. Even if the property is to be used for a most worthy purpose, the courts have held it to be *ultra vires* and void.

An Arizona case[30] involved lots one to ten inclusive of the City of Prescott, including a brick schoolhouse with four classrooms and an auditorium. The property had long been used for school purposes, but it had been leased to a hospital association a few months before suit was instituted. The term of the lease was for five years at an annual rental of one dollar, payable in advance. The lessee was granted the privilege of renewing it indefinitely for five-year periods upon the terms and conditions of the original lease, which stated an agreement to keep the building in repair and insured, to pay all light, power, water, and gas charges against the property, and not to allow any business to be conducted on the premises in violation of the law. In case the premises were totally destroyed the lease would be terminated. The Superior Court of Yavapai County, Arizona, ruled in favor of the Prescott School District when the Prescott Community Hospital Commission brought action for a declaratory judgment determining the validity of the executed lease. On appeal, the Supreme Court of Arizona affirmed the lower court's decision. The Supreme Court looked upon the lease as a gift of property to the association as long as it chose to use it, subject only to the conditions of keeping it in repair and assuming all service charges. The only way in which the lease could be terminated, said the court, would be through the total destruction of the property. The court said:

> It is doubtless true that the maintenance of a hospital in the city of Prescott is a most praiseworthy objective, and that contributions for that purpose by those individuals or organizations which are legally permitted to make them are most commendable but school districts are not permitted to give away the property of a district even for the most worthy purpose, and since it appears clearly by the terms of the lease that this is its practical effect, we hold that it is *ultra vires* and void.

30. *Prescott Community Hospital Commission* v. *Prescott School District No. 1 of Yavapai,* 57 Ariz. 492, 115 P. 2d 160 (1941).

Similarly, the Normandy School District of St. Louis County, Missouri, was not permitted to sell or lease or convey to the University of Missouri unneeded school property which the University planned to use in the formation of junior college districts. Action[31] was undertaken to compel the acting president of the board of directors of the local school district to execute a deed conveying property of a local school district to the University of Missouri, pursuant to a contract agreed to by the board excluding the president. Fred R. Small, duly elected, qualified and acting president of the Normandy School District, declared it was his duty to execute lawful and properly authorized conveyances of real estate on behalf of the district.

Facts state that the Normandy School District of St. Louis County comprises an area of approximately fifteen square miles with a population of approximately 52,000 people and twenty-six separate incorporated areas within its boundaries; that on September 20, 1958, the voters of the school district approved a $625,000 bond issue to enable district to purchase the property here involved; that the 128 acres, with the then existing improvements, were purchased in 1959; that the purchase price was $600,000; and that, when said bond issue was approved by the voters, it was determined that a tax of five cents per $100 valuation of real property for a period of twenty years would be necessary to retire said bonds; and that subsequent to the acquisition of the property by the school district, an increase in the value of real property within the district as determined by a re-assessment thereof, caused the tax to be reduced to 3.8 cents per $100 assessed valuation to retire said bonds in twenty years. There is no stipulation or other evidence as to the actual market value of the property on November 4, 1961.

It is further admitted "that the School Board, at a regularly called and duly held meeting on November 4, 1961, made determinations: (1) that the aforesaid property located at 8001 Natural Bridge Road in said School District is not required for the use of the School District, (2) that the said property could be used for purposes of offering education beyond grade twelve by an institution of higher education, and particularly by the University of Missouri, (3) that the taking over of the Junior College now designated as University

---

31. *State* v. *Small*, 356 S.W. 2d 864 (1962).

of Missouri — Normandy Residence Center by The Curators of the University of Missouri for use by it for its educational purposes would be of great and inestimable value to the residents of Normandy School District and to the youth residing therein and others seeking such advantages, (4) that it would be to the best educational interest of the Normandy School District to transfer the aforesaid property to The Curators of the University of Missouri for use in its educational purposes, (5) that the said written offer of The Curators of the University of Missouri then before the Board was fair and reasonable considering the educational and other advantages that would be afforded to the relator School District and the entire community, and (6) that said offer should be accepted."

The school board contended that the power of government and control vested in the school district by necessary implication includes the power *to permit the use of the land* for educational purposes by the State University, if the board of education of the school district shall have found that *the educational interests of the school district will be best served thereby.*

The court declared that nothing was presented relative to this which concerns a proposed sale and conveyance of property of the value of some $600,000 owned by the school district, but not required for the use of the district, to The Curators of the University of Missouri "for use in its educational purposes" for $60,000. The court further disagreed to this proposed sale of land when it stated:

> It is clear from the admitted facts that the proposed sale was not made after advertisement; that it was not made at public sale; that the sale was not to the highest bidder after advertisement; and that the parties are and have been proceeding on the basis of a private contract and private sale for a cash consideration not exceeding ten per cent of the cost of the property to the School District in 1959.

It is clear from the record that the alleged benefits to the school district — the difference between $60,000 and $600,000 — are entirely contingent upon the subsequent management, control and use of the property by the University, which in turn are contingent upon subsequent appropriation of funds by the legislature. Benefits for the transfer of land would come to the Normandy School District relative to the University of Missouri expanding its higher educational program only if the legislature in its wisdom and within its available resources approves this form of progress.

In making comment on this the court stated in conclusion:

The essential and decisive facts are that the District seeks to divest itself of title to the property in exchange for some ten per cent of its value without any attempted compliance with the applicable statutory provisions. This it cannot do, absent express legislative authority.

Briefly . . .

1. School districts attempting to lease — even for the most worthy purposes — property not required for school use, will be declared ultra vires and void without specific legislative authority.

9. School Board Permitting Use of Athletic Field to Group Not Connected with School

Litigation can arise when a school board permits an organization or group to use school property in a manner not directly connected with a program of the school, or when it is allegedly used for private purposes and such use is not public in nature.

In a Kansas case[32] action was brought by Elinor Nieman and others against Common School District No. 95, Butler County, Kansas, to enjoin the school board from making available the athletic field of a school district to any organization or group, when use is not directly or entirely connected with the athletic program of the school, or when use thereof in any manner will interfere with the plaintiffs' reasonable enjoyment of their property.

It was contended that the address system which was erected was of sufficient strength to cause the plaintiffs considerable annoyance; that lights were maintained in a way to illuminate their property to the extent that they were unable to sleep or rest or reasonably to enjoy their property while baseball games were conducted; that vehicles were parked about plaintiffs' property in such a manner as to deny plaintiffs' reasonable access to or egress from their property; that persons attending the games trespassed upon plaintiffs' property and that men and women used it in lieu of adequate toilet and sanitary facilities; and that dirt and dust were constantly being carried upon plaintiffs' property in such manner as to deny plaintiffs the beneficial use of the property.

The trial court granted a temporary injunction, but the Kansas Supreme Court ruled that the trial court had erroneously enjoined the school board from permitting the use of the athletic field to outside groups or organizations which proposed to conduct baseball games or exhibitions. The Supreme Court did agree, however, that the injunction should be granted against the use of the address system at ball games and against the continuance of using the field so as to produce dust which blows upon plaintiffs' property, and against the use of the flood lights later than 10 P.M. The court concluded, "Where athletic field is located on property owned by school district, management and control of such field is vested in officers of school board."

32. *Nieman* v. *Common School District No. 95, Butler County,* 171 K. 237, 246, 248, 232 P. 2d 422 (1951).

Briefly . . .

1. Where athletic field is located on property owned by school district, management and control of such field is vested in officers of school board.

Chapter Five

LITIGATION
RESULTING FROM
AFTER-HOURS USE

AS OUTSIDE USE of school property increased, opportunities likewise increased for challenging such use, with the result that court decisions were sought. A study of the appellate court decisions resulting from such actions reveals involvement in seven specific areas:

1. The use of public school property for fraternal meetings
2. The use of public school property for private school purposes
3. The use of public school property for public assemblies
4. The use of public school property for public or private dances
5. The use of public school property by religious organizations
6. The use of public school property for religious purposes
7. The use of public school property as a theatre run for profit

1. The Use of Public School Property for Fraternal Meetings

Some decisions of the courts relate more specifically to particular types of cultural and recreational uses of school facilities by the community. Lodges, granges and other clubs and fraternal groups have been prominent in American life, varying in type from rural to suburban to urban areas. In sparsely settled sections, where membership is scattered and distances are great, schoolhouses frequently are suggested as feasible meeting places for such organizations. And disputes have sometimes arisen concerning the use of these buildings for such meetings.

In an Illinois community William A. Lagow, a taxpayer, sought to restrain the board of school directors from permitting certain fraternal organizations to hold meetings in one room of the local school building.[1] The schoolhouse in question was a two-story brick structure with the first floor divided into two classrooms. The second floor contained one large assembly room and a small room designed as an office for the superintendent. Within ten years after the erection of the building, the school board found it unnecessary to use any part of the second floor. For a consideration amounting to about seventy-five dollars a year, the school directors permitted the Modern Woodmen, Odd Fellows and Royal Neighbors to hold their meetings in an upper room. This rental fee enabled the district to extend the school term from five to six months, and teachers testified that meetings of the fraternal orders in no way interfered with school activities or damaged the building. Injunction to prevent this use of the building was sought primarily on the ground that the directors had no authority to permit such use.

By statute the directors had control and supervision of schoolhouses and were permitted to "grant the temporary uses of schoolhouses when not occupied by schools, for religious meetings, Sunday schools, for evening schools and literary societies, and for such other meetings as the directors may deem proper." The Supreme Court of Illinois affirmed the decision of the trial court and held that directors, deriving their powers from the statute, were clearly within their powers in permitting the use indicated.

---

1. *Lagow* v. *Hill*, 238 Ill. 428, 87 N.E. 369, Affirming Judgment 143 Ill. App. 523 (1909).

A somewhat similar case[2] arose in Arkansas when modifications had been made in the stairway of a two-story school building in order to facilitate renting the upper story to a lodge. A statute specifically authorized school officials to permit a private school to be conducted there when the building was not needed for the public school. The plaintiff contended that since this use had been stipulated by statute, the district was in effect denied authority to allow other non-school uses.

There was offered in evidence a contract made between representatives of the local Odd Fellows Lodge and the directors of the district, under the terms of which, for the consideration of fifty dollars, the directors rented the second story of the school building for the use of the lodge for a term of one year, with an option to renew the lease for a period of five years. The school district, however, reserved the right to use the building for school exhibitions and entertainments of its own. At the annual election, the directors caused the question of ratification of this lease to be submitted, and it was ratified by a vote of nineteen to one.

In upholding the school board's action the court stated that in its management of school property it was the board's duty to make the most advantageous arrangement possible from the district's standpoint, that the rental was a significant item, that the arrangement would be void if it interfered with the use of the building for school purposes, and that in no case would the board divert school funds to construct a lodge building.

In its opinion, the court concluded:

> It is a matter of common knowledge that many quasi public uses are made of the rural school buildings of the state. We do not believe it was the purpose of the Legislature, in granting express authority for private schools to be taught in the public school building, to exclude other uses where such uses do not interfere with the schools nor injure the buildings.

A somewhat unique situation appeared in a Kansas case[3] involving the efforts of a woman's club to use school property. The Walker Community Ladies Club was interested in a meeting place, but the

---

2. *Cost* v. *Shinault,* 113 Ark. 19, 166 S.W. 740, Ann. Cas. 1916c, 483 (1914).
3. *Blankenship* v. *School District No. 28 of Wyandotte County,* 136 Kan. 313, 15 P. 2d 438 (1932).

school as it stood was not suitable. The club had about $600 which it desired to expend in the construction of an annex to the public schoolhouse. The district contributed $150, husbands of the club members contributed labor and businessmen of the area contributed materials. The annex was completed in the spring of the year, with the club furnishing a piano, chairs, a stage curtain, and other equipment. This annex was then used for club activities. It was also employed as a stage by the children in occasional programs.

Prior to construction of the annex, the district carried a $1,300 fire insurance policy on the building. After the annex was added, however, the policy was changed to one of $2,500, which the defendant district paid. The plaintiff carried a separate policy on the piano.

The schoolhouse was subsequently destroyed by fire, and the school district collected the insurance. The Walker Community Ladies Club laid claim to $1,200 of the amount collected. The club contended that when the annex was constructed the understanding was that it would remain club property, which the court remarked would have been beyond the authority of the school district if attempted. When complaint was made that the school district should pay for benefits received and retained, the court responded:

> The school district did not agree to pay for the annex. It did not agree to insure the annex for the benefit of the plaintiffs. It did not agree that, if the schoolhouse should be burned and the insurance collected, it would hand over part of the insurance money to plaintiffs.

The club received no insurance money. The powers of the school board are conferred by statute, and no statute could be cited. However, there seemed to be no objection to the club's use of the school property, along with normal school use, so long as the club did not attempt to assert ownership.

Briefly . . .

1. School boards have the authority to grant use of school facilities to fraternal organizations so long as such use in no way interferes with the schools nor injures the buildings.

2. There seems to be no objection to fraternal organizations being given permission to use school property along with school use so long as the organization does not attempt to assert ownership.

2. The Use of Public School Property for Private School Purposes

Situations have arisen which involve the maintenance of private schools on public school property. Courts have at times considered such use to be a preferred type of community use of public school facilities and have been lenient regarding it.

In 1949, in the state of New York, action[4] was taken by Thelma B. Schnepel and others against the Board of Education of the City of Rochester, to restrain the board of education from authorizing the giving of private dancing lessons in city public schools and from permitting use of the buildings for that purpose. The plaintiff sought action under a statute for school board acts constituting a waste of public money. The board claimed that under the same statute action could not be maintained, because the board members of the city are officers of a school district, and a school district is not a municipal corporation as stated in statute.

In dismissing the complaint the court said:

> The acts of the school board grow out of the exercise of powers either provided by the Education Law pertinent to the use of public school buildings and property inherent in its control over its teaching employees . . . Whether the subject activities permitted and authorized by the defendant are improper and illegal or the result of an exercise of discretion regarding which there may be an honest difference of opinion, is not a question to be considered here, for the reason that the Board of Education in so acting, whether rightfully or wrongfully, has exercised powers specifically reserved to the state in its control of public education; in these functions, the Board acts solely as an agent of the state.

In different perspective was an issue which arose in Arkansas during the economic depression of the 1930s. In this case[5] a school board had employed a superintendent and teachers for a period of six months, at the same time passing a resolution authorizing the teachers to operate a subscription school, and giving them the use of school equipment for a period of two months. There was some agreement or understanding between the board and teachers as to what should be

4. *Schnepel* v. *Board of Education of City of Rochester*, 195 Misc. 371, 89 N.Y.S. 2d 793, Affirmed 276 App. Div. 943, 94 N.Y.S. 2d 838 (1949).

5. *Burrow* v. *Pocahontas School District No. 19*, 190 Ark. 563, 79 S.W. 2d 1010 (1935).

charged by the teachers for the subscription school, but the board had nothing to do with the tuition so charged. After the school district had exhausted its funds for operation of the free public school, the teachers made an arrangement with the Arkansas Department of Education whereby the two-month tuition could be used to supplement the six-month free school in maintaining an *A* grade rating. The pupils were advised by the teachers that unless they attended the two-month subscription term, full-term credit and promotion certificates would not be granted.

Jessie W. Burrow had two children of school age, the tuition charge for these two being twenty dollars per month. He declined to pay the tuition fees imposed and brought suit to restrain the school board, the district, and the teachers from charging and collecting the tuition fee for the two-month school, demanding that his children be permitted to attend the school without payment of tuition.

The only question before the court related to the school directors' right to let the school building to the teachers for use as a tuition school after the expiration of the free school term. A statute provided:

> The directors of a school district may permit the use of the public schoolhouse thereof for social, civic, and recreational purposes, or any other community use including any lawful meetings of its citizens, provided such meetings do not interfere with the regular school work, and they may make a charge therefore if they deem it proper to do so.

The court upheld the school directors, defining the use of the building for a tuition school as a "community use":

> Certainly the conducting of a tuition school at which all the school children in the district were permitted to attend for a small consideration cannot be said not to be a community purpose. It is well known that during the last few years many school districts in the state have been without funds to operate a free public school for any considerable period of time, or for no time at all. If the directors should be without the authority to permit the operation of a tuition school, the children of such districts would be deprived of school privileges entirely or for such short periods of time as really to accomplish very little good.

Thus the court justified private school as a "community use" of school property.

Public and private agencies have at times cooperated in providing a building for public school use and perhaps for other concurrent uses by the community. A situation reflecting such joint public and private

i

effort was illustrated in a New Hampshire case[6] early in the century.

William H. Brooks and others sought to prevent the School District of Franconia from appropriating a sum of money for a plant to provide lighting for Dow Academy. Dow Academy was a private educational corporation originally established for the purpose of "maintaining a school in the town of Franconia . . . for the diffusion of knowledge in all the branches of academic education." The building was erected and furnished to accommodate all the students in the district, from the primary grades up, before the building burned. Later, the Academy trustees together with the district agreed to erect a new building suitable "to house all the schools of said district," provided the district would pay $4,500 to the treasurer of the Academy, the district "to have the use of the new building . . . on the same terms heretofore it has had the use of the old building." The public school students occupied three rooms in the new building, as they did in the old one. The other rooms were occupied by the Academy. Controversy apparently did not arise in connection with the $4,500, but arose subsequently with regard to funds voted for establishing a lighting plant in the Academy, when it was alleged that such use of funds constituted giving public funds to a private agency. The court ruled the appropriation was legal. Said the court:

> As the building was for all practical purposes its schoolhouse, the right of the district to expend money for repairs upon it cannot be doubted. The mere fact that the academy may incidentally derive a benefit from the money so expended is immaterial.

The court said that the Academy was not absolute owner of the property, but that it assumed the duties of a trustee to hold the property available to the district for all necessary district school purposes. Since light in the schoolrooms was necessary for accommodating the district's pupils, it could not be referred that the money was to be spent for a lighting plant not needed by the district.

Briefly . . .

1. A school board may permit the giving of private dance lessons in the public schools in that it exercises power either provided

6. *Brooks* v. *School District of Franconia*, 73 N.H. 263, 61 A. 127 (1905).

by the statute pertinent to the use of public school buildings and property or inherent in its control over its teaching employees. In these functions, a school board acts solely as an agent of the state.

2. A private school using public school facilities was justified as a community use of school property when a public schoolhouse was permitted to be operated for two months as a private school, following a six-month public school term, whereby children who could not afford to attend a private school received accreditation.

3. Public and private agencies may cooperate to provide facilities for public school use and for other concurrent uses by the community.

3. The Use of Public School Property for Public Assemblies

The extent to which school boards may permit or deny the use of school buildings for public assembly to non-school groups continues to be a troublesome question. It is the general rule that boards of education have the authority to permit such use of school buildings outside of school hours but under certain restrictions. The authority of boards of education is controlled by statute in many states.

A Missouri case[7] was governed by a statute authorizing the use of schoolhouses "for religious, literary or other public purposes . . . when such use shall be demanded by a majority of the voters of such district voting at an annual or special meeting where such question was submitted." The statute required that when a schoolhouse was so used "it shall be the duty of the party or parties using it to keep it clean and in good repair and to leave it in as good a condition as it was when they took charge of it," and provided that if the user should fail to comply with the foregoing provisions the directors "may refuse them further use of it until said provisions are complied with."

In this instance a literary society had been using the building pursuant to an authorizing vote, but the directors were dissatisfied, alleging that the building had not been left in a clean condition. The school board met in a store in the city of Nevada, a place outside the boundaries of the district, and made an order forbidding the literary society to use the schoolhouse.

Evidence showed, however, that the meetings had been orderly, and that the building had been left clean and in good repair, therefore the board could not close the schoolhouse to the society. The voters had granted the right to use it, and the board "was without authority to interfere with such use except on the statutory ground that the society had failed to leave the house in good repair and in a clean condition." Concurring, the court remarked:

> We think the meeting held by the board in Nevada was not a legal meeting and that the action there taken to deprive the society of the use of the schoolhouse was of no effect. The board of directors of the school is a body cloaked with authority to discharge such functions of public nature as are expressly prescribed by statute. It can exercise no power expressly conferred or fairly arising by necessary implication from those conferred. It can act only as a body and at meetings called or held in the manner

7. *State* v. *Kessler,* 136 Mo. App. 236, 117 S.W. 85 (1909).

and place provided or authorized by statute . . . Without any statutory enactment on the subject, it is obvious that considerations of public policy demand that the official meetings of public bodies be held within the limits of their territorial jurisdictions; otherwise, public servants might do in secret that which they would not want to attempt to do under public scrutiny, and thereby much injury might be done to the public welfare.

The raising of funds to provide a convenience for a permitted public assembly gave rise to an interesting case.[8] Citizens were inconvenienced at public assemblies by lack of lighting, heat and a bell, the schoolhouse being lighted by lamps the people brought from their homes. To provide the schoolhouse with a stove, lamps and a bell, the citizens organized a "box supper" at which a fund of $14.45 was raised by the sale of refreshments. By a vote of the meeting the fund was devoted to the purchase of the articles mentioned, and a committee was voted upon to take charge of the fund and to look after the purchases. The money was put into the hands of the defendant, W. H. H. Smith, a local merchant. Smith was to hold it as a "treasureman," subject to the order of the plaintiffs, to be spent by them for the specified articles, as Smith himself testified. When the plaintiffs demanded the money to make the purchases, he refused to give it up, on the ground that it should be spent in providing articles for a new schoolhouse which had been contemplated rather than for the old one. Action was then brought by the plaintiffs to recover the fund.

In its decision the court said that the plaintiffs had the right of action as trustees of the fund.

California has a very detailed and elaborate statute governing the use of school property for public assembly. It has what is designated as the Civic Center Act, an act which establishes a civic center at "each and every public school building and grounds within the State" and provides for the use of school facilities by all groups, with certain exceptions. Four California cases during the period 1941-1946 reveal the difficulties inherent in this type of statute.

The first of these cases,[9] in 1941, concerns a request made through

8. *Scribner* v. *Smith,* 104 Mo. App. 542, 79 S.W. 181 (1909).

9. *Goodman* v. *Board of Education of San Francisco Unified School District,* et al., 48 Cal. 2d 731, 120 P. 2d 665 (1941).

the Civil Liberties Union by Mrs. Lillian Goodman, representing the Socialist Party, for the use of the school auditorium to discuss the position of that party on peace. The meetings were to be open without admission charge to members of the group and to any other persons interested in discussing the topic.

The request was denied by the school board on the ground that a discussion of this nature violated a rule of the board prohibiting the use of a school building for sectarian, political or partisan purposes. Suit was brought to compel the Board of Education of San Francisco to permit the use requested.

The California Appellate Court held that permission to use the building must be granted, saying:

> The only discretionary power conferred upon the board is that it may deny permission to use the schoolhouse by subversive organizations, the burden of proving the character of affiliation of the group being upon the board. . . . If the board is unable to prove the subversive nature of the organization, then the schoolhouse may be used and the group may meet and discuss . . . all subjects and questions which in their judgment may appertain to the . . . interests of the citizens.

The statute in question permitted the use of school buildings for meetings to discuss subjects which in the judgment of interested persons pertained to the educational, political, economic, artistic, and moral interests of the citizens. And, although the statute used the permissive word *may* in describing the powers of boards in permitting non-school use of the buildings, the court construed the word *may* to mean *must,* thus making it mandatory upon boards to allow such use.

The second California case[10] arose in 1945. The court ruled in favor of a school board when the Payroll Guarantee Association, Inc., and others brought *mandamus* proceedings against the Board of Education of San Francisco Unified School District to compel the granting of an application to use a school auditorium for public assembly. The issue involved a request to use the auditorium for an open mass meeting to consider placing a proposed constitutional amendment on the ballot. Gerald L. K. Smith was the scheduled

10. *Payroll Guarantee Association* v. *Board of Education of San Francisco Unified School District,* 27 Cal. 2d 197, 163 P. 2d 433, 161 A.L.R. 1300 (1945).

speaker. Evidence was presented to indicate that at various places where Smith had spoken, picketing and noisy boisterous activities had accompanied the meeting, and there had been a declared intention to picket the proposed meeting if it was held. The school board rested its refusal of the request on the probability that evening classes meeting in the building would be disturbed, although such classes were not meeting in the auditorium itself. Petitioners seeking use of the auditorium stated that any disturbance which might result would not be of their own doing, that legislation existed for the police to handle such disturbances, and that they, the petitioners, should not be penalized for possible shortcomings of the police.

In upholding the board's refusal, the court emphasized the extent to which a speaker determines the character of a meeting and the importance of answering the peaceful use of school facilities for the school's primary purpose in contrast with other permitted but secondary uses. The court reasoned as follows:

> Speakers who express their opinions freely must run the risk of attracting opposition; they cannot expect their opponents to be silenced while they continue to speak freely. If a speaker in a school building or the opposition that he aroused attracted so much attention as to disturb school activities, it would not be for the police to curb those who incidentally caused the disturbance so long as their activities were lawful, but for the board to prevent the occurrence of such a disturbance. Neither a speaker nor his opponent are thereby stilled; they may express themselves fully and freely in school buildings as elsewhere whenever their activities do not bring in their wake a disturbance of the regular school program.
>
> The board's primary concern is with the maintenance of that program. It cannot dissipate its energies by seeking to guide and control or even to evaluate the strategy of opposing factions at every passing meeting that may be held in a school building. The activities of two opposed groups might operate in conjunction to interfere with school work. A speaker has a large part in fixing the character of his meeting. He cannot disclaim some share of the responsibility for whatever reactions his speech provokes. Again the disturbance might result, not from any activity of either the speaker or his opposition, but merely from an overflow audience. It is for the board to determine, not who would motivate a disturbance, but how serious is the risk of disturbance. The primary task of the schools is education. The statute established that the educational activities of schools shall at all times take precedence over other permissive but secondary uses of school buildings. In passing on an application for an extraneous use of a school auditorium the board must consider the probable effect of the proposed use of the regular school program and must deny one that would lead to an interference with that program.

A further 1945 dispute[11] followed as a sequel to the Payroll Guarantee Association case. The same group renewed its request to use the auditorium, changing the meeting place to a Sunday afternoon when no school classes were scheduled, but making no changes regarding the program or speaker. As a condition to being granted permission to use the school auditorium or gymnasium, the board required any organization seeking such use to furnish a public liability insurance policy to protect the district against damage claims for injury to persons while attending non-school meetings. The plaintiffs sought the use of a school auditorium without furnishing the public liability insurance policy, and the Supreme Court of California held they were legally entitled to use of the auditorium.

Two sections of the California Educational Code provide for "the use of schoolhouses granted free lighting, heating, janitor service, and other necessary expenses in connection with the use of public school buildings shall be provided for out of school funds." The court pointed out that the insurance policy withheld the use of buildings from those who were unable to procure insurance. Also, such requirement constituted a charge for the use, contrary to the statute.

Justice Carter in concurring remarked:

> The basis of the right of assembly is the substitution of the expression of opinion and belief by talk rather than force; and this means talk for all and by all . . . It has been said that: "Peace is a bell which prevents those who set it pealing from hearing any other sound." In the last analysis it is for the courts to declare the extent to which administrative power may be exercised in the light of the constitutional and statutory provisions fixing the limits of such power.

Dissenting, Justice Edmonds said:

> No one has an absolute right to hold a meeting in a public school, and the Legislature has declared that the use of any public schoolhouse and grounds "is subject to such reasonable rules and regulations as the governing board of the district as prescribed in the statutes." Free speech is one of our most cherished constitutional rights but it is subject to certain limitations. For example, as Mr. Justice Holmes laconically stated, the right of free speech does not permit one falsely to cry "fire" in a crowded theatre.

11. *Ellis* v. *Board of Education of San Francisco Unified School District,* 27 Cal. 2d 322, 164 P. 2d 1 (1945).

A state is free to permit or to withhold the use of school property for non-school community purposes; but if it makes its school buildings available for public meetings generally, it cannot arbitrarily withhold this privilege from any particular group of citizens.

Thus in a California case[12] a statute prohibited the use of school buildings by "subversive elements" — *i.e.*, by any person who was affiliated with an organization advocating the overthrow of the government of the United States by force. Acting under the authority of this statute, the board of education of the San Diego schools refused permission to the San Diego Civil Liberties Committee to use the school building for a meeting unless they signed the following oath:

> I do not advocate and I am not affiliated with any organization which advocates or has as its object or one of its objects the overthrow of the present government of the United States or of any State by force or violence, or other unlawful means.

Those seeking the use of the building refused to sign the oath, claiming it was a violation of their constitutional rights and, in so demanding it, the statute and the board rule violated these rights. Concurring with the San Diego Civil Liberties Committee, the court said:

> Freedom of speech and of peaceable assembly are protected by the First Amendment of the Constitution of the United States against infringement by Congress. They are likewise protected by the Fourteenth Amendment against infringement by state legislatures . . . However reprehensible a legislature may regard certain convictions or affiliations, it cannot forbid them if they present no "clear and present danger that they will bring about the substantial evils" that the Legislature has a right to prevent . . . Since the state cannot compel "subversive elements" directly to renounce their convictions and affiliations, it cannot make such a renunciation a condition of receiving the privilege of free assembly in a school building.

In New York a similar situation arose, again involving the use of school facilities by an unpopular group or by one espousing a somewhat unpopular cause.

The Board of Education of Yonkers has been plagued with this problem. In 1955 such a case[13] reached the Supreme Court of the

---

12. *Dankins* v. *San Diego Unified School District*, 28 Cal. 2d 536, 171 P. 885 (1946).

13. *Ellis* v. *Dixon*, 281 App. Div. 987, 120 N.Y.S. 2d 854, Appeal Denied 281 App. Div. 1037, 122 N.Y.S. 2d 384 (1955).

United States. It involved the refusal of the Board of Education of New York to permit a group known as the Committee for Peace to use school facilities for public assembly during after-school hours. The board gave no reason for its refusal to permit the use requested, apparently feeling it was under no obligation to explain its decision. The Supreme Court of the United States decided the case not on its merit but on procedural grounds, and dismissed the decision. Upon re-argument in the Supreme Court it appeared that the Committee for Peace had failed to lay sufficient foundation for a decision on a claim of denial of federal constitutional rights, and dismissal of this suit by the New York courts might have rested upon this adequate non-federal ground. Thus, the effect of the decision was to leave the ruling of the school board intact. It did quote, however, to the effect that any activity coming within the scope of school and community welfare should be allowed and encouraged through permitting the use of school buildings by outside groups. On the other hand, it emphasized the point that any activity should be rigidly debarred which is not embraced in the general school program and which is of a controversial nature liable to arouse ill feelings, jealousy and dissension, or to lead to misunderstanding. It further stated that nothing which would tend to foster intolerance, bigotry, animosity, or dissension should be allowed to inject itself into the public school system of the state.

Chief Justice Warren and Justices Black, Douglas and Clark dissented, believing that allegations were sufficient to state a case of discrimination.

In 1958 the same problem involving the same school district and organization again appeared before the courts.[14] Here again an organization known as the Yonkers Committee for Peace was denied the use of a school building because the board knew that other meetings of the organization had caused strife and dissension in the community. The Yonkers Committee for Peace accused the board of denying it the use of the building while permitting similar use by other groups

14. *Ellis* v. *Allen*, 165 N.Y.S. 2d 624, Appeal Dismissed 4 N.Y.S. 2d 693, 171 N.Y.S. 2d 86 (1958).

comparable to the organization in question, namely, the South West-chester Chapter of the Americans for Democratic Action, Lodge No. A, B'nai B'rith, and the Henry Jones State Lodge of the American Labor Party. Upon appeal to the State Commissioner of Education the action of the board was sustained, and action was brought to obtain a judicial review of the Commissioner's decision sustaining the board.

The discretionary power of a school board, as a legal rule, is not absolute. It may not deny to one organization the use of a school building and permit such use by other groups in the same category, all factors being reasonably equal. If the board chooses to close the door to all outside organizations it may do so, but if it opens the door to any *one,* it must treat alike *all* organizations in the same category.

The court held that the school board is not a censor and that its duty so far as school buildings are concerned is merely to regulate and to protect them. It may not deny the use of the buildings to an organization simply because it, or even a part of the public, may be hostile to the opinions or program of such an organization. However, if fair proof is presented that "a clear and present danger exists," and that public disorder and possible damage to the school property would result from the proposed use, then the board is within its power to deny such use. Justifiable exclusion is not discrimination. Whether such proof is possible would depend upon whether the evidence showed that other organizations in the same category had been permitted to use the buildings.

A case[15] in California illustrates how the authority of boards of education to permit the use of school buildings for public assembly outside school hours may be subject to express statutory limitation.

By provision of a California statute the school boards may not permit school buildings to be used for the commission of an act intended to further a program, the purpose of which is to overthrow the government of the United States by force, violence, or other unlawful means. An implementary statute requires any individual or group applying for the use of school property to deliver to the school board

15. *American Civil Liberties Union of Southern California* v. *Board of Education of City of Los Angeles,* 10 Cal. Reptr. 647, 359 P. 2d 45 (1961).

a Statement of Information to the effect that, to the best of the knowledge of the person signing the statement, the school property will not be used in violation of the statute. The constitutionality of this statute was considered by the Supreme Court of California in 1961. The American Civil Liberties Union applied for the use of certain school buildings in which to hold a series of meetings which would be open to the public. The application was denied because the American Civil Liberties Union refused to make and to deliver the required statement to the board. It contended that the requirement violated their rights and liberties under the Constitutions of both the United States and the State of California.

The constitutionality of the statute was upheld by the lower court, but this decision was reversed by the Supreme Court of California. The lower court held that the statute did not authorize school boards to forbid mere academic discussion of revolutionary doctrines in school buildings. Rather it permitted them to deny the use of buildings only for the commission of acts intended to further any program, the purpose of which was to overthrow the government by force. With this the California Supreme Court did not agree, stating that communist domination of an organization does not tend to prove that forbidden acts would be committed in a school building. In fact, it expressed the thought that acts of unlawful excitement were more likely to be committed secretly in carefully selected groups rather than in public meetings. It was fearful that efforts to protect the state from subversive acts could result in undue restrictions of the right of free speech and assembly.

In their dissenting opinion, adopted from that of the lower court, which was the underlying basis of the lower court's decision, Justices Schauer and McComb said:

> Courts may not bind themselves to reality nor are they justified in thinking from shadows. In this case we are faced with the stark reality of active subversive elements operating at our very doorstep, working diligently and tirelessly in fanatic devotion to dictates of our enemies. Through our legislature, the people of our state have declared and ordained that these self-same subversives shall not have access to the public school buildings of the state for the commission of acts of subversion. If this is not a just and proper exercise of free government, then we are indeed helpless as a state and as a nation. We cannot and we shall not brand this legislative mandate as "unconstitutional." To do so might appease those among us who still believe that terrorists and revolutionaries should be allowed free rein on the public domain until such time as the first shot is fired, but this myopic idealism can lead only to ultimate disaster. We believe that overthrow of the government by force is certainly a substantial

enough interest for the government to limit speech. Indeed, this is the ultimate value of any society, for if a society cannot protect its very structure from armed internal attacks, it must follow that no subordinate value can be protected.

The parties hereto are the same ones that were involved in another court case[16] in 1963. Again the American Civil Liberties Union sought to compel the board of education to approve its application for a permit to use the John Burroughs Junior High School auditorium for a series of bimonthly public meetings on the subject of "The Bill of Rights." The board of education refused the application upon the sole ground that the petitioners refused to file a Statement of Information as required by Rule 1316 of the Los Angeles Board:

> 1316. Statement of Information. Each person or group requesting the use of the premises for a Civic Center Activity shall, as a condition for the issuance of the permit, file the following statement:
> "The undersigned states that, to the best of his knowledge, the school property for the use of which application is hereby made will not be used for the commission of any act which is prohibited by law, or for the commission of any crime including, but not limited to, the crime specified in Sections 11400 and 11401 of the California Penal Code. I certify (or declare) under penalty of perjury that the foregoing is true and correct."

The sole question presented by this proceeding was whether the board of education had the legal right to make compliance with Rule 1316 a prerequisite to an otherwise lawful use of the school premises.

The use for which the school was requested was admittedly a proper use, within California's Civic Center Act (Chapter 4, Division 12, Education Code), which makes school property available for any public use which does not interfere with the school program. The refusal of the American Civil Liberties Union to comply with Rule 1316 was based solely on principle, in that they believed the requirements to be unconstitutional.

In the 1961 case (see page 97), the California Supreme Court declared that the Statement of Information required by Section 16565 was unconstitutional. This section reads as follows:

> The undersigned states that, to the best of his knowledge, the school property for use of which application is hereby made will not be used for the commission of any act intended to further any program or movement

16. *American Civil Liberties Union of Southern California* v. *Board of Education of City of Los Angeles,* 28 Cal. Reptr. 700, 379 P. 2d 4 (1963).

the purpose of which is to accomplish the overthrow of the Government of the United States by force, violence or other unlawful means:
   That ....,
the organization on whose behalf he is making application for use of school property, does not, to the best of his knowledge, advocate the overthrow of the Government of the United States or of the State of California by force, violence, or other unlawful means, and that, to the best of his knowledge, it is not a communist-action organization or communist-front organization required by law to be registered with the Attorney General of the United States. This statement is made under the penalties of perjury.

The tenor of that opinion was that the statutory requirement was aimed not at the use to which the school property would be put, but was intended to bar certain organizations because of their political beliefs — in other words, that the statute ignored the fact that such an organization might desire to use the property for perfectly legitimate purposes.

When that decision became final, the Board of Education for the City of Los Angeles investigated the necessity and propriety of filling (by local rule) the gap left by the California Supreme Court's holding that Section 16565 was unconstitutional. It noted that sections of the Civic Center Act prevented improper use of school property, while still other sections granted it the power to make local rules and regulations for such purpose. The board of education considered several proposed regulations and finally adopted Rule 1316. The American Civil Liberties Union failed to comply with the rule and sought remedy of the court.

The court failed to declare Rule 1316 unconstitutional. Justice Peters commented for the court:

> The rule does not require an applicant to divulge its political, sociological or economic beliefs. Neither does it require an applicant to set forth its general purposes, its associations, or anything about itself save and except the use to which it intends to put the school property — and even in that regard it makes no distinction between prospective uses so long as they are within the law.

On the same day and concurrent with the above decision the Supreme Court of California delivered an opinion[17] involving the same American Civil Liberties Union organization and the Board of Educa-

---

17. *American Civil Liberties Union* v. *Board of Education of the San Diego Unified School District,* 28 Cal. Reptr. 712, 379 P. 2d 16 (1963).

tion of the San Diego Unified School District. In January 1961 the Supreme Court of California directed the San Diego Unified School District to permit public meeting or meetings in any of their school buildings without requiring a Statement of Information in any form prescribed by Section 16565 of the California Education Code. As was previously noted this section of the California Code was declared unconstitutional.

In December 1961 "a revised procedure relating to application for use of school facilities" was adopted by the San Diego Unified School District. Thereupon the American Civil Liberties Union filed an application for the use of the Hoover High School auditorium to hold a series of meetings on the subject: "The Constitution and Civil Liberties."

The school board refused to act favorably upon such application solely because the American Civil Liberties Union refused to submit the executed questionnaire which was required as part of the "revised procedure." The American Civil Liberties Union sought *mandate* to compel the San Diego Unified School District to grant its application.

The California Supreme Court so ordered a *limited mandate* directing the board of education to act upon the application of the American Civil Liberties Union for use of the auditorium without requiring the questionnaire prescribed by the "revised procedure." Again the regulations here involved were declared unconstitutional.

By issuing a *limited mandate* the Supreme Court left open the opportunity for the San Diego Unified School Board and others to adopt proper regulations, within constitutional limitations, to make school property available to the public. The court stated:

> As a result of respondent's (San Diego Unified School District) apparent reluctance to abide by our prior decisions, there still exists, in San Diego, a vacuum in this important field of regulation. The interests of the public in school property are not being protected. In view of respondent's (San Diego Unified School District) action, we could order, by mandate, that respondent (San Diego Unified School District) grant the request of petitioner (American Civil Liberties Union) without further delay. But this we are not inclined to do. The interests that the public has in school property to have proper regulations adopted by local boards relating to such use is too great to be disregarded. Respondent (San Diego Unified School District) may now see fit to adopt proper regulations within constitutional limitations. It should be given another opportunity to do so. For that reason only a limited mandate will issue.

It can be assumed that other school districts in California will follow the pattern set by the Los Angeles School Board whose action in permitting public use of school facilities was suggested and advocated by the Supreme Court of California.

In New York the courts had to decide whether proceeds derived from conducting a benefit in a high school auditorium could be used as a legal defense fund for Freedom Riders, the question being whether proceeds used for such a fund came under "educational or charitable" purposes, as specified in the New York statute. There it is provided that the board may permit the use of a school building "for meetings, entertainments and occasions where admission fees are charged, when the proceeds thereof are to be expended for an educational or charitable purpose."

In this New York case[18] the court was asked to compel the Board of Education of Union Free School District No. 1 of the Town of Scarsdale to revoke a permit issued to the Westchester Committee for Freedom Riders, for the purpose of conducting a concert or benefit in the auditorium of the Scarsdale High School. The petitioners were residents and taxpayers of the school district. It was not disputed that admission fees were to be charged; the only question presented was whether the proceeds were to be expended for "an educational or charitable purpose" under the statute. From the pleadings it was shown that the proceeds of the meeting were to be used as a legal defense fund for Freedom Riders.

The court, holding that the defense of Freedom Riders was a charitable purpose, said:

> . . . It is important to keep in mind that the test prescribed in the statute is not whether the licensee itself is an educational or charitable organization, but whether the funds will be disbursed for an educational or charitable purpose. It seems reasonably plain to the Court that the purpose is charitable when the proceeds of the project are to be used in the defense of persons facing criminal charges and threatened with criminal penalties. Donations made to legal aid societies furnish a close parallel and few would deny that the contributions to such organizations are charitable in nature. In our concept of government the freedom of the individual is so jealously guarded that the donation of money toward his defense against criminal prosecution may be as important an act of charity as one that provides him with necessities of life. The Court therefore finds that the proceeds of this meeting will be expended for a charitable purpose.

18. *Dohrenwend* v. *Board of Education of Union Free School District No. 1,* 227 N.Y.S. 2d 505 (1962).

The court did not pass upon the question as to whether the board's action was wise or unwise. This determination was held to be in the board's discretion and not in the court's, questions of policy having been delegated to the school authorities by the legislature.

Leasing of school facilities for lectures sponsored by "controversial groups" continues to trouble school districts. In another New York case[19] the issue involved the use of the facilities of Hunter College of the City of New York; but many of the comments of the court are equally applicable to a public school system.

William F. Buckley, Jr., editor of *National Review,* a conservative magazine, and others brought suit to compel the authorities of Hunter College to allow him to lease college facilities for a series of forums. Similar forums had been held since 1954 on the college premises.

In June 1961 the Administrative Committee of the college promulgated a set of Policies Governing Use of Hunter College Facilities. This statement of policy provides that college facilities are "primarily for academic use," then goes on to specify permissible non-academic uses: First, student extra-curricular activities; second, activities of professional or academic organizations; third, educational conferences; and finally, the fourth, set forth as follows:

> Other programs offered by outside organizations insofar as these are determined to be compatible with the aims of Hunter College as a public institution of higher learning.

The policy statement goes on to say that this fourth criterion would not be met, "for example, by organizations whose meetings have caused disturbances; whose presence would tend to impair the good name or the academic prestige of the College; or whose character would give reasonable grounds for the assumption that the College favors particular groups or movements having a distinct point of view or position over other groups or movements opposed to their point of view or position."

Buckley and others contended that, although there is no obligation to make public schools available for non-academic uses, once they have been made available, the regulations governing use must meet

19. *Buckley* v. *Meng,* et al., 230 N.Y.S. 2d 924, 35 Misc. 2d 467 (1962).

constitutional standards — in particular, the First Amendment. To this, Hunter College authorities asserted that as long as the regulations "do not discriminate against a prospective tenant by refusing him while renting to others in the same category for the same use," there is no constitutional infirmity, and the regulations must be upheld.

Commenting that the regulations governing the use of Hunter facilities are either unconstitutionally vague or else embody an unconstitutional principle of selection, the court remarked:

> While there may be no duty to open the doors of the schoolhouses for use other than academic . . . once they are opened they must be opened under conditions consistent with constitutional principles. . . . A state is without power to impose an unconstitutional requirement as a condition for granting a privilege even though the privilege is the use of state property.
>
> The principle of these cases is the simple one that what the state cannot do directly it may not do indirectly. Since there is no power in the state to stifle minority opinion directly by forbidding its expression, it may not accomplish this same purpose by allowing its facilities to be used by proponents of majority opinion while denying them to dissenters.

Briefly . . .

1. Even though proposed use of the schoolhouse out of school hours is in itself legitimate, a board of education may find that community sentiment is divided as to propriety of the use and may properly refuse a request on grounds that granting a request will result in dissatisfaction and criticism.

2. Schoolhouses are not public places in the sense that use thereof may be demanded as a matter of right by any individual or organization for public or private discussions.

3. School authorities may, if they choose, close the door to all outside organizations, but if they open the door, they must treat alike all organizations in the same category.

4. Where school authorities elect to allow school buildings to be used for non-school purposes, their duty is to protect and regulate the building but not to act as censor, and they may not discriminate against any organization simply because they, or part of the public, are hostile to opinions or programs of such organization.

5. It is unconstitutional for a school district to grant use of

school property for non-school purposes by requiring an applicant to sign a statement that school property will not be used to seek to overthrow the government by force or violence, on the ground that the test of oath requirement abridges both the state and federal constitutional guarantees of freedom of speech and assembly.

6. Official meetings of public bodies must be held within limits of their territorial jurisdictions.

7. A school district has no interest in funds raised by citizens of a community to provide some convenience for public meetings in school buildings where permission to meet has been granted by a school board.

8. A board of education may not only make reasonable regulations with regard to use of school property for authorized purposes, but may deny an application if its use would further overthrow of the present government of the United States by force or violence or other unlawful means, or would interfere with the use and occupancy of public schoolhouse and grounds as required for purpose of public schools. The burden of proving the character of affiliation of the group lies upon the board of education.

9. A school board must consider the probable effect on the regular school program of permitting community use of school property and must deny any use that would lead to an interference with that program.

10. Local school boards cannot deny the use of school facilities because of failure of a group to comply with a board rule which requires an applicant to furnish public liability insurance in the name of the school district.

4. The Use of Public School Property for Public or Private Dances

In recent decades social dancing has become a more common form of recreation than it was in earlier years. However, the frequent use made today of the gymnasium or other parts of the school plant for social dancing does not mean that dancing has always been permitted in public school buildings. It is interesting to observe that the attitude of the courts on the legality of such use often changes as the attitude of the people changes.

A Utah court set forth a view[20] which may have been common about the turn of the century. School trustees proposed to lease a schoolhouse for public and private dances. It was contemplated that the seats, which had been fastened to the floor with screws, would be removed and temporarily stacked in the hallway outside the room to be used; ink from inkwells in the desks would be spilled during the stacking process; and, in any case, the room in question was regularly and necessarily used during the day for school purposes. A statute provided that the trustees "may permit a schoolhouse, when not occupied for school purposes, to be used for any purpose which will not interfere with the seating or other furniture or property; and shall make such charges for the use of the same as they may decide to be just, but for any such use or privilege the district shall not be at any expense for fuel or otherwise." The trustees contended that under the statute they might use the schoolhouse for public and private dances for young people of the district — the part of the building in controversy would accordingly be used for school during the day and for dances in the evening.

The court refused permission on two counts. The first related to the statute — that the use shall "not interfere with the seating or other furniture." "It is difficult to conceive," said the court, "how it would be possible to make a greater interference with the seating of the schoolhouse than that proposed by the trustees in this case." The other count related to public policy — using public property for a private purpose. So it appears that the court would not have permitted the use of the building for dancing, regardless of the interpretation of the statute. Since there was no authority to levy a tax to build a dance

20. *Lewis* v. *Bateman,* 26 Utah 434, 73 P. 509 (1903).

hall, the court said, "it necessarily follows that a board of trustees have no right . . . to, in effect, convert a public school building into a public or private dance hall."

Thirty years later, again in Utah, the court held that letting the school building for various outside uses, including dances to which admission was charged, did not violate a statute prohibiting the use of school buildings. The possibility that dances might be "detrimental to the schools" was not even hinted. The letter of the law in Utah had not been changed between the respective dates of these decisions.

In this case[21] the owner of a hall, in which were held dances and other entertainment, claimed that the business of his hall had materially decreased until it had become an unprofitable enterprise, claiming moreover that this condition was caused by the use of high school facilities for similar entertainment. School authorities had permitted the buildings and grounds to be used for a course of lyceum lectures, musical entertainments, dances, motion picture shows, football and basketball games, and other entertainment and activities, for many of which fees had been charged, and to which the general public had been invited by various schemes of advertising.

A lower court decision indicated that the entertainment and activities were private in nature and not part of the curriculum, that holding such entertainment to which admission was charged constituted a commercial use of the building, and that permitting such use without charging for fuel and other services violated the law. In overruling this decision the Supreme Court said:

> We must conclude that, while the conducting of a motion picture show, dances, and other entertainments, where an admission is charged, may have some business aspects, yet, in view of the word of our statute, we cannot say that the Legislature intended by the word "commercial" to exclude all games, dances, baseball, football, basketball, debates, lectures, or musical entertainments where a charge is made for admission to such entertainments. Entertainments of this nature cannot, in the presence of the well-known definition of the word, be said to be commercial, because there is no merchandise or commodity exchanged, bought or sold. . . . Where an admission fee has been charged, the profits, if any were obtained, have been uniformly and exclusively used, not for the enrichment of any

21. *Beard* v. *Board of Education of North Summit School District,* 81 Utah 51, 16 P. 2d 900 (1933).

person or group of persons, but for the purchase of accessories and equipment for use in the schools. . . . The element of a charge of an admission fee cannot be regarded as a determining factor as to whether a particular activity is commercial or not.

The court did remark in reference that the discretion to determine whether or not a school building will be used for such purposes is vested in the board of education and not in the courts. There are remedies available to citizens of a district who believe the board has acted unwisely or will so act in the future. One is by petition to the board, and the other by the election of new members. The exercise of discretion within legal limits will not be interfered with by courts except for compelling legal or equitable reasons where the board is clearly abusing the discretion vested in it.

In a California court case[22] the court recognized dancing in the school as a recreational activity. The vital point in the case was whether the board of education was authorized to permit a social dance in the high school building. In interpreting a statute which "provides a civic center at each and every public schoolhouse, where the citizens of the respective public school district . . . may engage in supervised recreational activities," the court said dancing would seem to be a form of recreational activity. Attention was called to the fact that *recreational* means "of or pertaining to or conducive to recreation." According to the *Century Dictionary, recreation* means "refreshment of strength and spirits, after toil; relief from toil or pain, diversion, amusement in sorrow or distress." In conclusion, the court said:

> We are inclined to believe that dancing is "amusement." If it were not, we very much doubt that it would be so popular. That it requires an "active movement" or "operation" and involves "physical" or "gymnastic" exercise, and that it frequently amounts to an "agile" performance, we think no one will dispute, who has witnessed a modern terpsichorean festival. Planting itself, therefore, on the definition of the terms used, the school board is not without warrant in asserting that this very diversion is one of the things contemplated by the Legislature for the social and educational activities of the community.

22. *McClure* v. *Board of Education of City of Visaba,* 176 P. 711, 38 Cal. App. 500 (1918).

A final case[23] illustrates the extent to which some school boards have gone in providing recreation which is both satisfying to youth and approved by parents, and also indicates the background from which social dancing came to be included in the recreational program. In summarizing the history of recreational activity in the school building and the precautions relative to dancing, Judge Paine, who spoke for the court, noted several community uses which were being made of the school building, and then described the conditions under which dancing was permitted.

> The evidence discloses that, during the voting of bonds for the construction of said building over twelve years ago, one of the arguments advanced was that said high school building would contain a large assembly room to be used for school and community purposes; that said building had in it a large assembly room or auditorium . . . which had been used upon over 1,000 nights for every sort of athletic, social, patriotic and recreational purpose; that among the uses to which it had been put have been lectures, parties, institutes, community choruses, minstrel shows, theatrical entertainments, and during the war for every form of patriotic advancement. . . . For each and all of these events, lights and janitor service, as well as heat in the winter time, was furnished by the taxpayers of the school district; and the board of education received applications from some of the parents to permit supervised dancing to keep their children from attending the public dances with their miscellaneous crowds and no supervision; and that vigorous protests came in from other parents who objected to dancing in any form of recreation and asked the board to prohibit the same; that long and careful study and discussion was given to the matter by the board during a period of several years, and at last the board decided to permit dancing under three general rules with minor conditions as follows:
> First. No general policy permitting dancing in the auditorium would be allowed by the board of education. Second. No dancing would be permitted at any function attended by all students. Third. Dancing would be permitted for one and one-half hours under the following conditions: Written permission must be obtained from the secretary of the board of education. It must be announced in advance that there would be dancing at the party. Members of the board of education must be present. The welfare board should always be invited. There must be some program other than dancing to occupy the evening.

The court cited a statute which authorized school boards to permit buildings to be used "for public assemblages," under board regulations, and which authorized boards to exact rentals to cover the added expenses involved. It was pointed out that in our high schools we have provided laboratories for the various physical and biological sciences, facilities for home economics and manual training, large auditoriums with stage apparatus, gymnasiums with baths and swimming pools,

23. *Brooks* v. *Elder,* 108 Neb. 761, 189 N.W. 284 (1922).

and athletic parks and amphitheatres of large seating capacity that bring and accommodate the crowds which attend football and other games. In upholding board action the court added:

> Yet some parents can be found who object to each and all of the things. In spite of this the public schools have constantly grown in power and influence in both city and country and have in many instances, become the one great community center for wholesome entertainment for all. During the past year the city of North Platte has enrolled one out of every ten of its inhabitants in its night schools, where gray-haired men attend classes with children in their teens. Meeting the demands of its community is the burden placed upon school officers. One of these demands of recent years is for supervised dancing to which parents, who desire it, may send their children. This demand arose at North Platte; the board of education considered it carefully for several years and finally decided to grant the use of the school building under rules therein set out, which are not open to criticism and which meet the hearty approval of the parents of the children attending.

Briefly . . .

1. A Utah court, thirty years later, held that letting the school building for various outside activities, including dances to which admission was charged, does not violate a statute prohibiting the use of school buildings.

2. Dancing in the public school is recognized as a recreational activity.

5. The Use of Public School Property by Religious Organizations

Even though a statute may prohibit a school board from extending the use of school property to religious groups, the courts will at times circumvent the statute and permit such use.

Confusion as to the group using a building as contrasted with the specific use being made of it was reflected in an Iowa case.[24] Action was brought to enjoin the school board from permitting a Jewish Federation, a corporation organized not for pecuniary profit, to occupy and to use a vacant school building and its adjacent grounds as a community center. The building and grounds were not being used for school purposes, and the board leased the premises for five years at a monthly rental of $100, with a provision allowing the district to cancel the lease upon six months notice if it decided to reopen school in the building or if the Federation misused the premises. The Federation had spent $4,000 in renovating the property, and the uses being made of it did not interfere with the educational opportunity of the pupils in the district. It was shown that the question of the leasing of the school property to the Jewish Federation was not submitted to the electors of the school district for determination, and they were not given an opportunity to vote on whether this lease should have been made.

The trial court held that the school board did not have the right to lease the property to the Federation and cancelled the previously executed lease. However, it permitted the Federation to continue to occupy the school building, holding that the Federation was not a group or organization which could be denied the right to use school buildings.

The community center maintained by the Federation was open to public use without regard to race, color or creed. It included a well-equipped library for general public use, weekly public forums, a teenage center, playground activities for neighborhood children during the summer vacations, and classes in Jewish history and language for Jewish children, with no religious instruction.

It was contended that the Federation was using the premises for religious purposes and that such use should not be permitted. The

24. *McLang* v. *Harper*, 236 Iowa 1006, 20 N.W. 2d 454 (1945).

Supreme Court of Iowa dismissed the contention and upheld the lease agreement, saying:

> Under statute, directors of the school district were unauthorized to lease vacant school buildings to society to be used for community purposes without submitting question to electors . . . . Evidence that work being done by Jewish organization in vacant school building with permission of directors of school district was of a community nature, and that Community Center, as operated by organization, was open to the general public, established that organization was not one which could be denied right to use school building on grounds that building was being used for sectarian religious purposes . . . It is our conclusion that the building is being utilized in a way that will result in a benefit to those who make use of it for community purposes and will also result in an indirect benefit to the entire community.

Briefly . . .

1. Even though the question of leasing school property to a religious organization was not submitted to the electorate for their approval, as stated in a statute, a school board was permitted to do so because the property was being utilized in a way that would result in a benefit to those making use of it for community purposes and would result in an indirect benefit to the entire community.

6. The Use of Public School Property for Religious Purposes

Religious groups have figured more prominently in disputes over the use of school property than any other private agencies. During the early part of the colonial history of the United States, communities had erected a single building to serve both as schoolhouse and meeting-house, as well as for religious meetings. As communities grew in wealth and population, more elaborate and often separate facilities for religious and educational purposes were provided, and the courts were confronted with the task of unraveling the intertwined rights of the different agencies.

Efforts to compel school authorities to allow religious groups the use of school property involved land which at an earlier date was granted for both school and religious purposes; or a building which was constructed from funds designated for dual use, and after such dual use had been made of the property for a time, the religious use lapsed. Two cases warrant consideration.

In one of these[25] land was transferred by trust deed for church purposes, with the provision that "after these conditions the trustees may build schoolhouses." With the consent of the trustees of the grant the school directors constructed a building on the land, using $640.75 of tax funds and $150 of subscription money. It was agreed with the trustees of the grant and stated in the subscription document that the building would be controlled by the school directors and would be used for both school and religious purposes when school was being held therein. When used for religious purposes, however, desks were damaged, as well as books, pencils and other items of school equipment. Accordingly the directors forbade the use of the building for religious meetings.

The Supreme Court of Arkansas reversed the decree of the lower court; and Justice Hughes, speaking for the court, said:

> The statute provides that "the directors shall have the care and custody of the schoolhouse, and grounds, the books, records, papers, and other property belonging to the district, and shall carefully preserve the same preventing waste and damage." It appears in this case that by the use of the schoolhouse for religious worship the seats were being damaged, and the books, pencils, etc., of the school children were being injured by

---

25. *Boyd* v. *Mitchell*, 62 S.W. 61, 69 Ark. 202 (1901).

persons attending the meetings for religious worship. In the exercise of their power of control, and their duty to preserve the property of the district, the school directors of this district did right, we think, in prohibiting the use of the schoolhouse for religious meetings.

A similar case[26] appeared in Illinois. Land was granted to five persons (as Trustees of Bethel Church) and their successors in office, to be used for school purposes. Before any use was made of this land the church disbanded, and several of its members, including four of the five trustees, joined the Church of Christ. The latter group erected a building on the property, this building being used for both church and school purposes until it burned down. The following year the school district voted to construct a new building on the premises, using tax revenue to pay for it. At that time no representatives of either of the foregoing church groups claimed any right of the land. The building was used jointly for school and church purposes, until the school directors decided not to allow further religious use of the building. Church trustees instituted suit to recover possession of the premises and on several occasions forcibly entered the building.

The court held that under the circumstances the building was obviously school property within the meaning of a statute which provided that directors should control and supervise district school-houses, further stating that when any schoolhouse was not needed for school purposes the directors might temporarily permit religious or other use. The court added that the religious organization had no right to use the schoolhouse without the permission of the directors, and that any occupancy which the church had enjoyed in the past was permissive and of such character that the directors might revoke it at any time.

Expressed or implied in some cases is the idea that religious use of a public school building infers using tax money to support a place of worship in contradiction of the federal or state constitution. In a Nebraska case[27] John W. Gilbert and John M. Simmons filed a

26. *School Directors* v. *Toll,* 149 Ill. App. 541 (1909).
27. *State* ex rel. *Gilbert* v. *Dilley,* 95 Nebraska 527, 145 N.W. 999, 50 L.R.A. (N.S.) 1182 (1914).

petition to compel the district school board to keep the schoolhouse closed to the public as a place of worship. The grounds were that the respondents had converted the schoolhouse into a place of worship against their consent and contrary to constitutional provision that:

> All persons have a natural and indefensible right to worship Almighty God according to the dictates of their own conscience. No person shall be compelled to attend, erect or support any place of worship against his consent or no preference shall be given by law to any religious society. Nor shall any interference with the rights of conscience be permitted.

On four occasions during the five years preceding the suit the schoolhouse had been used for religious meetings without interference to school work. The Supreme Court of Nebraska rejected the allegation that the use of the school for religious meetings amounted to using tax revenue to support a church. If the relators, said the court, had shown that the schoolhouse had been used for religious meetings to such an extent as to make it a place of worship, or if they had been compelled to pay anything for the erection, support or repairs of the building for that purpose, one might hold that they were entitled to the relief demanded.

It is interesting to note in this case that the court considered religion analogous to geography, astronomy, philosophy or agriculture:

> If the school officers should see fit to use the building for the purpose of hearing a lecture on geography, illustrated by maps and charts, there probably could be no good objection. If the lecture should be upon astronomy or any kindred educational subject, there could not well be any serious objection . . . It is the opinion of the writer that to impart knowledge concerning religion and religious subjects is educational to the extent that our civilization covers and includes those subjects. I am unable to see that religion is so far removed from the general purpose of a school as not to be tolerated in a moderate degree. Religion is a part of our civilization. It is therefore, of necessity, part of our education. An intelligent discussion of religion and its kindred subjects approximate as nearly to the ordinary use of a schoolhouse as its use for the purpose of receiving a lecture on geography, philosophy, history or agriculture.

A New York case[28] is significant because of the distinction drawn between religious meetings as such and meetings held by religious

---

28. *Lewis* v. *Board of Education of City of New York,* 157 Misc. 520, 285 N.Y.S. 164, Affirmed 247 App. Div. 106, 286 N.Y.S. 174 (1937).

organizations where the meetings themselves are not religious in character. By statute, school boards had the custody and control of school facilities, and were authorized to permit their use, when not needed for school purposes:

> For holding social, civic and recreational meetings and entertainments, and other uses pertaining to the welfare of the community; but such meetings, entertainments and uses shall be non-exclusive and shall be open to the general public.
> For meetings, entertainments and occasions where admission fees are charged, when the proceeds thereof are to be expended for an educational or charitable purpose; but such use shall not be permitted if such meetings, entertainments and occasions are under the exclusive control, and the said proceeds are to be applied for the benefit of a society, association or organization of a religious sect or denomination.

Among the groups permitted to use buildings were Catholic Newman Clubs, Young Men's Christian Associations, Young Women's Christian Associations, Hi-Y Clubs, and various Jewish organizations. The school board said that the facilities were used for "ethical educational and cultural discourses and lectures for the moral uplift of the pupils in the public schools," and that at no time were they used for inculcating "the tenets of any religious denomination or for any meeting or purpose, directly or indirectly, in which any denominational tenet or doctrine is taught." When a taxpayer complained that the buildings were being devoted to a religious use, the court replied that the weakness of the complaint lay in confusing the racial and religious affiliations of the users with the uses being made of the buildings. The court noted that in the United States all racial and religious groups were equal before the law, and that no distinction could be made between believers and non-believers.

In upholding the use being made of the buildings, the court continued:

> A sect or tenet which is intolerant of those of a different sect or tenet is the precise antithesis of religious liberty. Freedom is negated if it does not comprehend freedom for those who believe as well as those who disbelieve. The law is astute and zealous in seeing to it that all religious beliefs or disbeliefs be given unfettered expression. Authentic free thinking involves the indubitable right to believe in God, as well as the unfettered license not to believe or to disbelieve in a Deity.
> To examine into the sectarianism of those seeking access to public school buildings would make it a travesty of our glorified liberty of conscience. Liberty for non-believers in God, but denial to believers in a Deity would be a mock of liberty.
> Rather than inimical to the educational policy of the state, or subversive of legitimate use, it is a wholesome thing to have the school buildings, which are maintained at large expense by the taxpayers, used

for the purposes and by the groups whose expulsion is here sought.
It is the use to which school buildings are put and not the identity of
the users, that is decisive of the lawfulness of the use.

A more recent phase of this controversy appears in connection
with "released-time" programs. Under these programs public school
pupils whose parents so request and consent may be released from a
certain amount of school time in order to receive such denominational
instruction as their parents designate. This religious instruction is
sometimes given in the schoolhouse by church personnel. Hence, the
extent to which public facilities may be used for this purpose has been
decided in an Illinois case.[29]

In 1940 members of the Jewish, Catholic and Protestant faiths
formed the Champaign Council on Religious Education, and secured
permission from the school board to offer religious instruction to public
school pupils in grades four to nine, providing parents signed printed
cards requesting that their children be permitted to attend. Weekly
meetings were held — thirty minutes for the lower grades and forty-
five minutes for the upper. The Council employed and paid teachers
for this purpose, subject to the approval and supervision of the superintendent of schools. Classes were taught by Protestant teachers,
Catholic priests and a Jewish rabbi, and conducted in regular school
classrooms. Pupils who did not attend these classes were required to
leave their classrooms and pursue their secular studies elsewhere in the
school building; pupils released from secular duties were required to
attend classes in religion. Attendance at these religious classes was to
be reported to the secular teachers.

It was contended that public funds were expended in the additional use of school buildings for independent religious instruction, a use
prohibited by statute. The State Supreme Court of Illinois ruled,
however, that this was not in violation of the statute and further said,
"Religious and religious worship are not so placid under the ban of
constitution that they may not be allowed to become the recipient of
any incidental benefit whatsoever from the public bodies or authorities
of the state." To its answer that the board cannot exercise any power

29. *People* ex rel. *McCollum* v. *Board of Education of School District No.
71,* 396 Ill. 14, 71 N.E. 2d 161 reversed, on other grounds 68 S. Ct. 461, 333 U.S.
203, 92 L.Ed. 648, 2 A.L.R. 2d 1338 (1947).

except in the manner provided by statute, the Illinois State Supreme Court elaborated in saying:

> It is, of course, true the board of education cannot exercise any power except in the manner provided in the statute, but that always presents the difficult question as to whether or not, under the existing facts, it has improperly exercised a power not in any manner provided by such statute. Apparently, the board here worked out a plan for religious education classes and by the plan it was not necessary for the schoolhouse to be occupied for any other purpose at that particular time. Further, these classes were so arranged as not to conflict with others. This arrangement, coupled with the rule that the courts will not interfere with the judgment of the board unless it has abused its power would not seem a violation of the power which the board was permitted to exercise . . . Our government very wisely refuses to recognize a specific religion, but this cannot mean that the government does not recognize or subscribe to religious ideas. The government does not recognize a particular faith but this does not mean that it is indifferent to religious faith. To deny the existence of religious motivation is to deny the inspiration of authority of the Constitution itself.

The United States Supreme Court reversed the decision with Justice Black, delivering the opinion of the court, saying:

> Facts indicate the use of tax supported property for religious instruction and the close cooperation between the school authorities and the religious council in promoting religious education. Pupils compelled by law to go to school for secular education are released in part from their legal duty upon the condition that they attend the religious classes. This is beyond all question a utilization of the tax-established and tax-supported public school system to aid religious groups to spread their faith . . . The state also affords sectarian groups an invaluable aid in that it helps to provide pupils for their religious classes through the use of the state compulsory public school machinery.

Justice Frankfurter, in concurring, stated rather succinctly:

> We renew our conviction that we have staked the very existence of our country on the faith that complete separation between the state and religion is best for the state and best for religion . . . If nowhere else, in the relation between Church and State, good fences make good neighbors.

Two appellate court cases reveal *mandamus* proceedings by which members of Jehovah's Witnesses sought permission to use school property when permission was denied.

In one of these cases,[30] the Jehovah's Witnesses were denied use

---

30. *State* ex rel. *Greisinger* v. *Grand Rapids Board of Education,* 88 Ohio App. 364, 100 N.E. 2d 294 (1949).

of the Grand Rapids High School auditorium for religious meetings and sought a writ of *mandamus* to compel the board to issue it. The court of appeals affirmed the lower court, holding that the board's refusal of an application of a religious sect, comprised of members who were not citizens of the community involved and whose tenets were not consonant with principles of good citizenship as taught by the schools, was not abuse of discretion.

In affirming judgment, the Court of Appeals of Ohio stated that the language employed in the statutes clearly evinces the intention of the legislature to grant a board of education discretionary power. The court called attention particularly to such phrases as "in its discretion, may authorize," "for any lawful purposes," "in any way interferes with the public schools," "any responsible organization," "leading to the development of personal character," "civic welfare," "shall prescribe such rules and regulations," "For . . . religious . . . meetings," and "as may make for the welfare of the community."

The court of appeals further commented that there was no evidence of any formal application on the part of any organization for the use of the school building. The applications in this case were made orally and in writing by individuals in varying groups and at different times, whereas the statute contains the following clause: "Upon application . . . of a group of at least seven citizens." The word *group* is significant. It imports a number of persons acting as one, and at the same time, for a common purpose. The group may make formal written application or the application may be oral, but it must consist of at least seven before such application may receive favorable action.

The other case[31] involved the right of members of Jehovah's Witnesses to use the auditorium of a Pittsburgh high school for a series of Bible lectures. The board denied a permit to the organization, and a writ of *mandamus* was sought to compel the board to issue it. The Pennsylvania statute provides that the board of school directors may permit the use of school facilities for "social, recreational, and other proper purposes, under such rules and regulations as the board may

31. *McKnight* v. *Board of Education*, 365 Pa. 422, 76 A. 2d 207, Appeal Dismissed 71 S. Ct. 737, U.S. 913, 95 L.Ed. 1349 (1950).

adopt." The Board of Public Education of Pittsburgh had adopted a rule which provided that "Permits shall not be granted to anyone for any religious or sectarian purpose," and denied the permit under this rule.

The Witnesses contended that denying them while permitting others the use of the auditorium constituted arbitrary and illegal discrimination against them. The writ of *mandamus* was denied. According to the court:

> Whether the school property shall be used by any group at all is a matter resting within the discretion of each board of school directors. This court is not a superboard of school directors in performance of an official duty. The legislature has delegated this power to the school boards, not to the courts. In the absence of any proof of unreasonableness or an arbitrary or capricious exercise of the power, the judgment of the board must stand.

Since the Witnesses were unable to prove any "unreasonableness or an arbitrary or capricious exercise of the power," they were unsuccessful in their suit.

The court made a point of the fact that there was no showing that the board had accorded the use of the building to others for religious use while denying it to the Witnesses. In other words, no other religious or sectarian group had been accorded treatment any different from that accorded the Witnesses; all religious groups were treated alike. Thus, board regulation which differentiates among groups is *not* arbitrary or unreasonable, but one which differentiates among organizations *within* a group, *is* arbitrary and unreasonable. To illustrate, the board may permit lodges to use the buildings, but deny that privilege to church groups. It cannot, however, differentiate among churches or among lodges.

A most unusual case[32] involving the use of school property for religious purposes concerned the erection of a nativity scene on a school lawn. In 1957 a committee known as the Creche Committee, composed of Catholics, Protestants and Jews, was formed to collect funds and erect a nativity scene in the Village of Ossining, New York. It was granted permission by the board of education to erect the scene

32. *Baer* v. *Kolmorgen,* 181 N.Y.S. 2d 230 (1958).

on the lawn of the junior-senior high school. A condition of the permission was that it would be erected and maintained only while school was not in session during the Christmas vacation.

Suit was brought by a group of citizens to enjoin the carrying out of the project. They contended that it violated the First and Fourteenth Amendments of the United States Constitution and a similar section of the Constitution of New York. The evidence showed that the scene was not erected or displayed while school was in session. It was also established that no public funds were expended, nor was the time of any public employee involved in the project. Incidentally, in 1956 this same nativity scene was displayed, but no court action resulted.

The suit for injunction was dismissed. In commenting on Jefferson's reference to "a wall of separation" between Church and State, the court said that this expression had received so much attention that one would almost think it was to be found somewhere in the Constitution. According to the court, there are two general bases for attacking a statute on the ground that it violates the Constitutional provisions cited above. First: Where a person is required to submit to some religious rite or instruction or is deprived or threatened with deprivation of his freedom for resisting that unconstitutional requirement. Second: Where a person is deprived of property for unconstitutional purposes, such as a direct or indirect tax to support a religious establishment. Concerning the Creche the court said:

> The Creche is undoubtedly a religious symbol. In viewing it, however, we are all free to interpret its meaning according to our own religious faith. If any public body were to limit that freedom or if any public institution were to give instruction as to its meaning there would, unquestionably, be a constitutional violation. That, however, is not this case. Here the School Board has done no more than to make a portion of its property available for the display. To that extent they have accommodated a religious, though non-denominational, group. However, the accommodation of religious groups is not *per se* unconstitutional. If such accommodation violates the doctrine of absolute separation between Church and State, then it is time that the doctrine be discarded once and for all.

The question of constitutional authority of school boards in permitting religious use of school buildings again arose in a case[33] decided

---

33. *Southside Estates Baptist Church* v. *Board of Trustees, School Tax District No. 1, In and For Duval County, Florida,* 115 So. 2d 697 (1959).

by the Supreme Court of Florida. Here the board had permitted several churches to use various school buildings during Sunday non-school hours. The use was temporary pending the construction of certain church buildings. It is not shown whether the religious groups paid rent or whether the school trustees incurred any direct expense in connection with this use. Certain taxpayers brought suit against the board of trustees to enjoin the temporary use of the public school buildings for religious meetings. Unsuccessful in the lower court, the taxpayers appealed.

The section of the Constitution of Florida applicable to this case is as follows:

> No preference shall be given by law to any church, sect or mode of worship and no money shall ever be taken from the public treasury direct-ly or indirectly in aid of any church, sect or religious denomination or in aid of any sectarian institution.

The Florida statute applicable provides in part:

> Subject to law, trustees of any district may provide for or permit the use of school buildings and grounds within the district, out of school hours during the school term, or during vacation, for any legal assembly.

It was the contention of the taxpayers that by permitting the religious groups to use the school buildings on Sundays the trustees, contrary to the constitutional provision quoted above, were indirectly taking money from the public treasury in aid of a religious denomination. It was their position that regardless of how small the amount might be, if anything of value could be traced from the public agency to the religious organization, the constitution had been violated. The trustees, on the other hand, insisted that the statutory provision quoted above granted them the discretion to permit the use of school buildings out of school hours "for any legal assembly," a designation that would include religious meetings. They also insisted that any indirect expense to the public stemming from depreciation of the buildings due to church usage was of such small consequence that the law should refuse to notice it. However, although the taxpayers apparently did not stress the point, it might be argued with some reason that even if religious meetings are legal assemblies under the statute, the churches are, in fact, being aided "directly or indirectly," contrary to the constitution.

Briefly . . .

1. In the exercise of their power of control, and their duty to preserve the property of the district, school authorities may prohibit worship in the school, where it is shown that school property is damaged, notwithstanding that the school was erected on land conveyed to school authorities for the purpose of religious worship.

2. A religious organization has no lawful right to use a public schoolhouse without permission of the directors, even though a schoolhouse, financed by tax revenue, was erected on land belonging to said religious organization.

3. A schoolhouse may be used for religious meetings where the religious services do not interfere with the use of the building as a school, where they are so infrequent as not to turn the building into a place of worship, and impose no burden of expense on the taxpayer.

4. The court of Nebraska considered religion analogous to geography, astronomy, philosophy, and agriculture.

5. It is the use to which school buildings are put and not the identity of the users, that is decisive of the lawfulness of the use.

6. Tax-established and tax-supported public school systems cannot be utilized to aid religious groups.

7. Board regulations which differentiate among groups are not arbitrary or unreasonable, but those which differentiate among organizations within a group are arbitrary and unreasonable.

8. The accommodation of religious groups is not per se unconstitutional when a school board makes a portion of its property available for a religious display.

9. School authorities have power to exercise reasonable discretion in permitting use of school buildings during non-school hours for any legal assembly, which includes religious meetings, subject to judicial review, should such discretion be abused to a point that it could be construed as a contribution of public funds to aid a particular religious group.

7. The Use of Public School Property as a Theatre Run for Profit

Sometimes the use of school facilities involves a school auditorium being employed as a theatre, in a manner quite different from the cultural and recreational uses usually permitted. Such activities may be attacked because of alleged "commercial purposes" and the school's becoming involved in fields of service already cultivated by private agencies.

Such a case[34] occurred in North Dakota. R. W. Simmons brought action to enjoin the board of education from renting the auditorium of the high school building for theatrical entertainments. Mr. Simmons was a stockholder in, and the manager of, the Auditorium Theatre Company, a corporation engaged in the business of operating a theatre in the city of Crosby.

The district court rendered judgment that the school board be enjoined and restrained from renting the high school auditorium to any "traveling troupes, persons, corporations and others who make a business of putting on community entertainments for profit," but the decree applied only to professional entertainers and was not to be considered as restraining anyone connected with the school or its classes, Chautauquas, local entertainments, athletic contests or non-professional entertainers.

After the trial court had made its determination in this case, the legislature set at rest all doubt as to the power of the board of education in this regard by enacting the following statute:

> School Boards and Boards of Education having charge of any school buildings may permit the use thereof, when not occupied for school purposes, under careful restrictions for any proper purpose, provided that such use shall not be at any cost to the district, and provided that furniture fastened to the building shall not be removed or unfastened. Public school or high school auditoriums and gymnasiums may be let for individual meetings, entertainments, or conventions of any kind, subject to such restrictions as the governing board of such districts shall prescribe, provided that such letting shall not interfere with the operation of school or with school activities, and provided that a charge shall be made for such use, at least sufficient to cover any cost to the district for light, heat, janitor service, or other incidental expense connected therewith.

The legislature had indicated that it was not certain but that this

---

34. *Simmons* v. *Board of Education of City of Crosby,* 61 N.D. 212, 237 N.W. 700 (1931).

power already existed, but that the statute was enacted to remove any doubt as to the existence of such power.

The Supreme Court of North Dakota reversed the trial court's decision with the following comment:

> The defendant school district has unquestioned power to rent the high school auditorium for the purposes and in the circumstances, shown by the evidence in this case. The permanent injunction rendered in this case contravenes the provisions of the statute. While, of course, the statute did not affect the rights of the parties at the time the judgment was entered, it does affect the right of the plaintiff to a permanent injunction this time and requires that such injunction be set aside. For "an injunction will be dissolved where, subsequent to its issuance, a statute which legalizes the acts restrained is enacted."

Briefly . . .

1. An injunction will be dissolved where, subsequent to its issuance, a statute which legalizes the acts restrained is enacted.

Chapter Six

THE
WRITTEN
POLICY

A NECESSITY FOR efficient operation of any school system is a written statement of board regulations concerning the after-hours use of school property. In fact, such a statement of policy could be a most essential step since the public is now putting considerable pressure on school boards for greater utilization of school facilities which have been provided by tax moneys.

Written policies are needed for answering the frequent problems that arise from day to day, for prompt approval in granting or denying requests, for achieving consistency and uniformity of procedures, for providing continuity in practice, and for settling the disputes that may develop when requests for the use of school facilities are submitted to the board.

In approaching the task of formulating a policy perhaps there is need to define what a policy is. A practical definition of a policy is merely to say it is "a way of dealing with a matter that is likely to arise frequently." Another way of defining policy may be to state that it is a guide for discretionary action. It must be narrow enough to give clear guidance to the chief school administrator as he makes decisions, but it must also be broad enough to enable him to use his own discretion in making decisions. It must provide room for him to maneuver as necessary in meeting the circumstances of individual requests.

Policy-making is the responsibility of the board of education. A policy is the board's way of saying what it would do if it were sitting behind the chief school administrator's desk all day long. Naturally the board cannot always be present and so it cannot know the many knots the school executive is constantly being called upon to untangle. By means of a policy the board tells him what to do, yet must not tie his hands completely.

In giving the chief school administrator a working set of rules to follow with respect to the extended use of school property, the following must be included: types of activities permitted, groups permitted, procedures involved in application, personnel policies as to operation and maintenance, rental and other fees charged.

In all cases, the school board reserves the right to renew, alter or revoke permits, or to deny use of property for good cause. The board is responsible for reasonable wear and protection and may insist on protective features such as insurance. It may also reserve the right to assume no obligation during use. The board also authorizes the preparation and administration of the necessary application forms, schedules, and reporting forms for custodians or other personnel.

The extent to which school property is used for non-school purposes appears to be directly related to the availability of school employees and payment for their services. In the past, school personnel have been expected to be available at the school building at any time it is used. As a matter of fact, many boards in smaller communities still adopt this view.

This point of view, however, is undergoing rapid change. Although administrative personnel may still be present on most of these occasions, it has become good practice to have a staff member, such as an assistant superintendent or a teacher, supervise these after-hours activities with a corresponding adjustment in work and pay schedule.

Operation and maintenance employees should not be expected to perform additional assignments unless additional compensation is made. As a result, it has become good practice to work out a schedule for additional compensation, usually on an hourly basis, for such supplementary services. Rates of pay according to Marcus W. Davies* vary from $1.00 to $3.00 per hour, with a median of $1.71 per hour for custodians and $2.58 per hour for engineers. In some instances, flat rates are agreed upon. In other instances, salaries and wages include supervision and participation in such extended services. Variations in fees depend upon the type and extent of activity, such as rehearsals or general use of auditorium and rest rooms. The use of school equipment, such as a motion-picture projector, has become a problem in many instances because of careless use. Additional charges are often made for such items of school property. Rentals received usually cover the cost of services but do not necessarily include the cost of heat, light, and ordinary wear-and-tear.

School personnel frequently called into service for these activities include custodians, engineers, stage crews, audio-visual operators, teachers and extra help.

As the concept of a true community school gains headway in the United States, accompanied by its extended use for all types of community activities, the problems of operation, maintenance, and personnel, together with additional costs, will mount. Obviously, boards of education will have to give this matter continued and thorough consideration, establishing policies which will be fair not only to the school administration, and to its operational and maintenance personnel, but also to the public they serve.

---

* Marcus W. Davies, "Extended Use of Plant Facilities," unpublished doctoral dissertation, University of Pittsburgh, 1956.

GATEWAY UNION SCHOOL DISTRICT
MONROEVILLE, PENNSYLVANIA
[furnished by Dr. Carl A. Newman, Supervising Principal]

RULES AND REGULATIONS GOVERNING THE USE
OF SCHOOL FACILITIES

1. Application for the use of school facilities included in the attached schedule must be presented in writing in duplicate on the district's formal application form.
2. All applications must be approved by the Board of School Directors; the Supervising Principal and the Union Board Secretary are authorized to approve requests for use of school facilities not included in the attached schedule.
3. The Board reserves the right to reject any application.
4. *Smoking is NOT permitted in any part of the building.*
5. Spectators and participants will not be permitted in rooms or other parts of the building not included in this agreement.
6. Rental rates include the service of one (1) janitor until 11 :00 P.M. for all school buildings with the exception of Gateway Senior High School which will be until 12 :00 o'clock midnight. Additional time will mean additional charges. Janitorial fees will be charged to all organizations, whether profit making or non-profit making for requests for use of school facilities on Saturdays.
7. Rental of the auditorium includes the use of the stage and auditorium only.
8. Rental of the gymnasium includes the use of the main floor and bleachers only. If dressing rooms and showers are requested an additional fee of $5.00 for each locker room.
9. Rental of old gymnasiums include the use of the main floor and bleachers only.
10. Three students (official stage crew) will be assigned to each program and must be paid separately from the rental fee. The rate will be a minimum of $2.50 per boy or $1.00 per hour, whichever is greater.
    Please note: These boys are responsible for the lights, sound equipment, microphones, curtains and school-owned props. They do not participate in loading and unloading for the program, but may help arrange stage settings and work during the program on the operation of the equipment.

11. The Lessee shall pay the owner for any damage done to the building or to the school equipment during the rental period.
12. The Lessee shall assign capable persons to report any disturbances to the Police Department and to control admissions.
13. The District shall under no circumstances be liable for injuries sustained by any person or to any property of the Lessee.
14. The above rates [see following] shall apply without exception to all applications for permission to use the school facilities.
15. Board Policy does *not* permit rental of school facilities on Sundays.
16. Make all checks payable to the Secretary, Gateway Union School District.

SCHEDULE OF RATES
FOR RENTAL OF SCHOOL FACILITIES

| | | GYMNASIUMS | | AUDITORIUMS | | |
| | | New | Old | New | Old | |
	All Purpose Rooms	Gateway MJHS South	Pitcairn Patton Hgts.	Gateway MJHS	Pitcairn Patton Hgts.	Classrooms
1. School sponsored organizations, clubs, PTAs and Community Recreation	Free	Free	Free	Free	Free	Free
2. Community organizations non-profit, civic and welfare	$ 6	$20	Free	$40	$10	Free
3. Community organizations when admission is charged or collection taken	$20	$30	$20	$50	$20	$ 5
3(a). Rehearsals or practice sessions for plays, recitals, etc.	$ 6	$20	Free	$40	$10	Free

4. Swimming Pool — $10 per hour plus $5 per hour for each locker room.

ABOVE RATES APPLICABLE DURING REGULAR SCHOOL YEAR, EXCEPT SATURDAYS AND HOLIDAYS WHEN JANITORIAL FEES WILL BE CHARGED.
Adopted December 11, 1963

RULES AND REGULATIONS REGARDING USE OF
GATEWAY SENIOR HIGH SCHOOL ATHLETIC FIELD
— OTHER THAN FOR SCHOOL ACTIVITIES

1. $10.00 per hour rental; Locker Room Rental — $5.00 per hour
   Minimum of 2 hours
   Maximum — Activity to cease prior to 11:00 o'clock
   $15.00 per hour rental if field lights are used.

2. Applicant must register name of at least one person as responsible
   for activity.

3. Must provide constant and adequate supervision, *i.e.,* police,
   auxiliary police, etc.

4. *All* parking to be on parking lot south of athletic field.

5. No traffic to be moved around high school building.

6. Provide own tickets, ticket takers, concessions, concession sales-
   men, etc.

7. Full details of program to be presented to Athletic Director and
   High School Principal one week prior to event.

BETHPAGE PUBLIC SCHOOLS
BETHPAGE, LONG ISLAND, NEW YORK
[furnished by Dr. Charles H. Bryan, Superintendent of Schools]

BETHPAGE SCHOOLS
Union Free School District No. 21
Bethpage, N.Y.

REQUEST FOR USE OF SCHOOL FACILITIES AND/OR AUTHORIZATION

(Please Print or Type)

Date _____

Gentlemen:

The undersigned requests approval for use of the Bethpage School facilities as indicated below:

NAME OF ORGANIZATION _____

TYPE OF ORGANIZATION _____
(Civic, Social, Recreational, etc.)

FACILITIES REQUESTED: (Check facilities listed below, indicating first and second choices by putting "1" and "2" next to your selection.)

SCHOOL		ROOM		EQUIPMENT REQUESTED	
Bloomingdale	____	All Purpose	____	Chairs (No.)	____
Broadway Jr. High	____	Auditorium (Jr. & Sr. High)	____	Microphone	____
Central Blvd.	____	Cafeteria (Jr. & Sr. High)	____	Phonograph	____
Charles Campagne	____	Classroom	____	Projector	____
Cherry Ave. - Sr. High	____	Faculty Room	____	Screen	____
Kramer Lane	____	Gymnasium	____	Tables (No.)	____
Pine Avenue	____	Other _____		Other _____	

DAY OF WEEK _____ DATES: FROM _____ TO _____

HOURS: FROM _____ TO _____ NO. OF ATTENDEES _____

PURPOSE (Give specific purpose) _____

If Admission Fee is to be charged, state specifically what proceeds are to be expended for:

_____

I have received and read the Bethpage Board of Education Policy and State Education Law relating to out of hours use of school buildings and accept responsibility for meeting the requirements stated therein.

Approved   ( )
Disapproved ( ) _____

_____
Signature of Applicant   Authorizing Official

_____
Address

Charge for) Registration Fee $_____
this permit) Room Charge $_____
               Extras $_____
_____   Total $_____
Telephone Number

Applicant's Copy

DPBRq-1-62

[Reverse side of application on preceding page]

EDUCATION LAW — Section 414 of Article 9 — Use of schoolhouse and grounds out of school hours.

Schoolhouses and the grounds connected therewith and all property belonging to the district shall be in the custody and under the control and supervision of the trustees or board of education of the district. The trustees or board of education may adopt reasonable regulation for the use of such schoolhouses, grounds or other property, when not in use for school purposes, for such other public purposes as are herein provided. Such regulations shall not conflict with the provisions of this chapter and shall conform to the purposes and intent of this section and shall be subject to review on appeal to the commissioner of education as provided by law. The trustees or board of education of each district may, subject to regulations adopted as above provided, permit the use of the schoolhouse and rooms therein, and the grounds and other property of the district, when not in use for school purposes, for any of the following purposes:

1. For the purpose of instruction in any branch of education, learning or the arts.

2. For public library purposes, subject to the provisions of this chapter, or as stations of public libraries.

3. For holding social, civic and recreational meetings and entertainments, and other uses pertaining to the welfare of the community; but such meetings, entertainment and uses shall be nonexclusive and shall be open to the general public.

4. For meetings, entertainments and occasions where admission fees are charged, when the proceeds thereof are to be expended for an educational or charitable purpose; but such use shall not be permitted if such meetings, entertainments and occasions are under the exclusive control, and the said proceeds are to be applied for the benefit of a society, association or organization of a religious sect or denomination, or of a fraternal, secret or exclusive society or organization other than organizations of veterans of the military, naval and marine service of the United States and organizations of volunteer firemen.

5. For polling places for holding primaries and elections and for the registration of voters and for holding political meetings. But no political meetings shall be permitted unless authorized by a vote of a district meeting, held as provided by law, or, in cities by the board of education thereof. Except in cities, it shall be the duty of the trustees or board of education to call a special meeting for such purpose upon the petition of at least ten per centum of the qualified electors of the district. Authority so granted shall continue until revoked in like manner and by the same body as granted.

6. For civic forums and community centers. Upon the petition of at least twenty-five citizens residing within the district or city, the trustees or board of education in each school district or city shall organize and conduct community centers for civic purposes, and civic forums in the several school districts and cities, to promote and advance principles of Americanism among the residents of the state. The Trustees or board of education in each school district or city, when organizing such community centers or civic forums, shall provide funds for the maintenance and support of such community centers and civic forums, and shall prescribe regulations for their conduct and supervision, provided that nothing herein contained shall prohibit the trustees of such school district or the board of education to prescribe and adopt rules and regulations to make such community centers or civic forums self-supporting as far as practicable. Such community centers and civic forums shall be at all times under the control of the trustees or board of education in each school district or city, and shall be nonexclusive and open to the general public.

NEW YORK STATE CONSTITUTION — Section 4 — Article 11.

Neither the state nor any sub-division thereof shall use its property or credit or any public money, or authorize or permit either to be used, directly or indirectly, in aid or maintenance, other than for examination or inspection, of any school or institution of learning wholly or in part under the control or direction of any religious denomination, or in which any denomination tenet or doctrine is taught, but the Legislature may provide for the transportation of children to and from any school or institution of learning.

BETHPAGE SCHOOLS
Union Free School District No. 21
Bethpage, N.Y.

Date _____

To: Building Principal _____ School
From: Office of Business Manager
Subject: Use of Building Change or Cancellation

The following change in use of your building has been made for:

_____
Name of Organization

CHANGE OF: Date _____   Time _____   Room _____
           From: _____
           To: _____

CANCELLATION: Dates: _____

           _____
           Time: _____
           Room: _____

Please retain this copy for your files:

Principal's Copy

DPBRq. 2-62

BETHPAGE SCHOOLS
Union Free School District No. 21
Bethpage, N.Y.

_____
Date

Dear

    This invoice is submitted for the use of Bethpage School District premises and/or

property on _____
Date(s)

for _____
Name of Organization

Room Charge:

_____ , _____
Room   School

for _____ , @ _____ ea. -- $_____
No. of times

Custodian: _____ , @ _____ ea. -- $_____
No. of Hrs.

Matron: _____ , @ _____ ea. -- $_____

               TOTAL DUE   -- $_____

_____
Edward W. Lavin
Business Manager

PLEASE MAKE CHECK PAYABLE TO UNION FREE SCHOOL DISTRICT No. 21

User's Copy

DPBI-1-62

Community Use of School Facilities

Policy:

The Board of Education authorizes the Superintendent and/or his designees to permit the use of School facilities by responsible community groups in the Union Free School District No. 21, when such use is consistent with Section No. 414 of Article 9 of the Education Law and Section 4, Article 11 of New York State Constitution. The School Administration is further authorized to establish rates for the rental of school facilities to other than school groups or organizations with direct school connections or organizations of a semi-educational nature.

Rules and Regulations:

1. Regular day school activities will have first priority for all space; adult education will have second priority; approved non-school groups will have third priority and will be assigned space according to the order of the receipt of their application.
2. Time of occupancy should terminate at 11:00 P.M. unless the user's permit indicates that prior arrangements have been made for payment of added custodial overtime costs. The use of indoor facilities is limited to Monday through Friday on the regular scheduled rates. Uses on Saturday, Sunday and holidays will be assessed regular rates plus additional overtime cost for custodial service.
3. Applications for use of school facilities should be submitted thirty (30) days prior to the anticipated use. Registration fees must accompany the application in the case of groups first request. Payment of rental fees according to the schedule of rates in this policy. Rental payments will be billed the using organization immediately after use. Early application for use of space is desirable.
4. Cancellations should be made by a using organization at least twenty-four (24) hours in advance. If costs are incurred by the School System due to cancellations without the twenty-four (24) hour notice, the actual costs involved will be billed to the organization. In the event of cancellation by the School System, notice of such cancellation will be given as far in advance of the actual time the property was to be used by the permittee, as possible. The Board of Education reserves the right to make such cancellations

in cases of emergency at any time without liability therefor.

5. Any activity carried on in school facilities shall be according to New York State Law and in conformity with Village and Town Ordinances and the dignity and moral standards associated with public schools. No meeting shall be held in a school building:

    a. for the purpose of advancing any doctrine or theory subversive to the State of New York or the United States of America

    b. for the purpose of advocating social or political violence, or which is of a nature likely to incite such violence.

6. The Board of Education, because of its responsibility for protecting the school districts buildings and property therein, may restrict rental of space with buildings to certain times and areas. It may also revoke a permit at any time and must have free access to all rooms at all times. When schools are closed for severe storms, scheduled community use will automatically be cancelled.

7. Special rooms equipment, or requests for installation of movement of furniture or equipment in conjunction with an organization's use of a school facility should be requested at the time the space is reserved. Such permission must be so stated on the permit.

8. Using organizations should abide by the regulations at each facility regarding no smoking. No alcoholic beverages are to be brought or consumed in school buildings or grounds. Nothing shall be sold, given, exhibited, or displayed without prior permission.

9. Organizations receiving permission to use school facilities are responsible for the conduct of both participants and spectators. Adequate provisions should be made to handle anticipated crowds.

10. Admission charges to activities held in school facilities shall be made only as stated by the user upon the application. Non-school groups sponsoring or presenting programs for which admission is charged are required to file a copy of the statement to the Collector of Internal Revenue with the office of the Superintendent. The Board of Education will not be liable for the payment of any taxes due on admission charges.

11. No commercial use of the Bethpage School Buildings, nor catering service by the Cafeteria Organization shall be permitted.

Procedure:

All permits for the use of school facilities shall be restricted to responsible organizations or adult individuals within the school district under the provisions outlined in this policy. Applicants must satisfy the issuing officer that they represent responsible local organizations, that they will guarantee orderly behavior and will underwrite any damage due to their use of the premises.

Eligibility as outlined in the policy statements above for non-school users will be determined at the time a representative of a using organization makes application for permit for use of a school facility. Questionable applications as outlined above will be referred to the Board of Education for final consideration.

Five (5) copies of the application will be completed by the applicant. Upon approval, the copies will be distributed as follows:

>   1 copy to the applicant to present to the custodian at the facility to be used.
>   1 copy to the Principal of the school.
>   1 copy to the Superintendent of Buildings and Grounds.
>   1 copy to the Building Custodian.
>   1 copy for the files in the Business Office.

Above form will include extra equipment or service required by the user.

Payment for space to be used will be billed immediately after use of the building.

Administrative Policy for Non-School Use of Bethpage Public Schools and Related Facilities

Purpose:

The purpose of this policy is to establish the eligibility of groups or organization who may be allowed to use the facilities under the supervision of the Board of Education of Union Free School District No. 21, the purpose for which these facilities shall be used, the regulations which govern such use, and the rates which shall be charged.

Authority:

Authority for this policy is derived from Section No. 414, Article 9 of the Education Law of the State of New York and Article 11, Section 4 of New York State Constitution.

Classification of Groups:

Class I: Organizations directly connected to School District No. 21 for the conducting of Business Meetings. These groups include School sponsored activities, PTA's, Teacher Organizations, Board appointed Citizen Advisory Committees and others as Board may direct.

Class II: Organizations which are educational in nature, but not sponsored by the School District, such as Creative Workshop, etc.

Class III: Organizations of a service and/or semi-educational nature such as Boy Scouts, Police Boys' Club, Dads' Club, Kiwanis, Rotary, etc.

Class IV: Organizations whose program is essentially social, civic, or recreational in nature (*i.e.,* entertainment, social and recreational functions of the PTA's, Civic Associations, etc.).

Class V: Exempted organizations, such as Service Organizations, Fire Department, Board of Elections, etc.

Admission Fees:

Any organization, in any classification, which charges an Admission Fee for its activity, shall be charged a room fee and a custodial overtime fee.

CLASSIFICATIONS AND ROOM/SERVICE RATES

Classification of Rates:

Classifications	Registration Fee	Room Charge	Additional Overtime For Custodial Service
I	0	0	0
IIA (Children's Use Only)	0	0	0
IIB (Adult Use)	$5.00	0	Schedule B below
IIIA (Children's Use Only)	0	0	0
IIIB (Adult Use)	$5.00	0	Schedule B below
IV	$5.00	Schedule A	Schedule B below
V	$5.00	0	Schedule B below

Schedule of Rates:

A. Classrooms $ 3.00
   All Purpose Room   5.00
   Elementary Gymnasium   5.00
   High School Little Theater   5.00
* Jr. and Sr. High Cafeteria   5.00
   Jr. High Gymnasium   15.00
   Sr. High Gymnasium   15.00
   Jr. High Auditorium   15.00
   Sr. High Auditorium   25.00

B. If *extra* Custodian is needed on duty on weekdays between 4:00-11:00 P.M. the charge is $2.50 per hr.
Weekdays — beyond 11:00 P.M. — $3.50 per hr.
Saturday, Sunday and Holidays — $3.50 per hr.

Note: Stage lighting and P.A. System in the Jr. and Sr. High School Auditorium necessitates Custodial Service and will be chargeable for plays or activities (including rehearsals for same) at the rate of $3.50 per hr.

* Special request must be made for kitchen facilities, which if approved, will require Cafeteria Employee to be present for supervision of equipment. The charge for said employee will be as follows:
Weekdays — $2.00 per hr.
Saturday, Sunday and Holidays — $3.00 per hr.

MONTGOMERY COUNTY PUBLIC SCHOOLS
ROCKVILLE, MARYLAND
[furnished by Mr. Paul A. Henry, Director of School Services]

APPLICATION FOR USE OF SCHOOL FACILITIES
BOARD OF EDUCATION
MONTGOMERY COUNTY, MARYLAND

THIS FORM MUST BE SUBMITTED AT LEAST ONE WEEK PRIOR TO DATE OF USE

NAME OF SCHOOL_____

Type Space Requested　　　　ALL-
and Number of Each: CLASSROOMS____;PURPOSE ROOMS___;CAFETERIA___;GYMS___;KITCHEN____
　　　　　　　　OR_____
TIME:____A.M. (OR)____P.M.: THRU:____A.M. (OR)____P.M.　NUMBER OF PERSONS EXPECTED__

　　　　In signing this application, the person representing the group or organization certifies to the Board of Education the following:

1. That he has been authorized by the group or organization to represent it.
2. That the "Regulations For The Use of School Buildings and Grounds" approved
　by the Board of Education have been read, are understood and will be
　complied with.
　　　　Payment of charges (check or money order made payable to the _school_ being
used) must accompany this application. Payments may be made in advance for all
future meetings.

NAME OF NON-PROFIT GROUP OR ORGANIZATION APPLYING_____

NAME OF PERSON REPRESENTING THE GROUP
　OR ORGANIZATION_____TITLE_____
　　　　　　　　　PRINT
SIGNATURE OF PERSON REPRESENTING THE GROUP OR ORGANIZATION_____

ADDRESS OF PERSON REPRESENTING THE GROUP
　OR ORGANIZATION_____TELEPHONE NO._____

DATES REQUESTED	BUILDING CHARGE	CUSTODIAL CHARGE	CHARGES FOR CAFETERIA WORKER	TOTAL CHARGES	FOR SCHOOL USE ONLY		
					No. HOURS	DATE PAID	AMOUNT
————							
————	SAME						
————	SAME						
————	SAME						

Use separate line for each date requested

INFORMATION BELOW TO BE FILLED IN BY PERSONNEL OF SCHOOL

COPIES TO
　ORIGINAL TO THE GROUP OR ORGANIZATION
　GREEN COPY TO DIRECTOR OF OPERATIONS,
　　BOARD OF EDUCATION, ROCKVILLE, MD.
　　(TO BE FORWARDED BY THE PRINCIPAL)
　PINK COPY TO DIRECTOR OF PUBLIC SAFETY,
　　COUNTY BUILDING, MONTGOMERY COUNTY, MD.
　　(TO BE FORWARDED BY THE PRINCIPAL)
　BLUE COPY TO CUSTODIAN
　YELLOW COPY TO BE FILED AT SCHOOL

_____
Approval of　　Date　Group
　Princ. or Vice　　Classification
　Principal　　　　(A or B)

　　　　　　　　(over)

[Reverse side of application on preceding page]

In submitting this application the applying group or organization is certifying that:

1. The group or organization using the school property shall save the County, the School Board, the individual members thereof, and any school officials or employees (free and without harm) from any loss, damage, liability or expense that may arise during, or be caused in any way by such use or occupancy of school property.

2. The group or organization does not limit membership in or attendance at its activities on the basis of race or color.

REGULATIONS FOR THE USE OF SCHOOL BUILDINGS AND GROUNDS
OUTSIDE OF REGULAR SCHOOL HOURS

Effective July 11, 1961
Amended October 9, 1961

The Board of Education approves and encourages maximum use of school facilities. The schools, when not used for public school purposes, are to be made available to approved county groups.

I. *Limitations of Use*

A. Since the Board of Education is charged by law with responsibility for school facilities, it must reserve the final right to deny the use of school facilities when the Board deems it necessary in the public interest.

Indicative of the guidelines the Board of Education will use in interpreting "the public interest" are:

1. that sponsoring organizations will conduct orderly meetings and further, such gatherings will not be of a nature to incite others to disorder;

2. that sponsoring organizations will conduct meetings which are not abusive of other groups by reason of race, creed or color.

B. All school buildings and grounds are to be used for educational, civic, social, religious, recreational, and similar activities by approved non-profit groups of citizens or organizations within the county.

C. No public school buildings or grounds shall be used for a purpose which is unlawful.

D. Gambling, the playing of bingo or other games of chance, raffles and lotteries are prohibited. The use of alcoholic beverages in school buildings or on school grounds is also prohibited.

E. There shall be no smoking in school buildings unless the area is posted otherwise.

F. School gyms shall be used for dances by the following groups only:

1. public school groups

2. dances under the auspices of organized recreation departments which groups shall assume financial responsibility for any damages resulting from the dances.

G. School buildings shall not be used for parties or celebrations which are essentially private in nature — this exclusion includes birthday, anniversary, and other similar parties.

H. All adult recreation programs (such as square dancing, folk dancing, etc.) must be sponsored by an organized public recreation department where the services of such recreation departments are available.

I. The schools shall not be used for recitals or exhibitions by private teachers of music or dancing, etc.

J. There shall be no signs, banners, pennants, etc. placed in or on school buildings or on school grounds by any group except those associated with activities sponsored by the school or the school PTA. Activities carried on in the schools by the Supervisors of Elections Office shall also be free of this restriction.

K. No group shall be eligible to use school buildings or grounds unless at least 2/3 of its membership is comprised of residents of Montgomery County.

L. No group which limits membership in or attendance at its activities on the basis of race or color shall be allowed to use school buildings or grounds.

II. *Application for Use*
   A. Permission
      1. Permission to use school buildings and grounds is to be granted by the following:
         a. For Elementary Schools: The Principal
         b. For Secondary Schools: The Principal
      2. If the Principal is not available, contact shall be made with the Director of Operations in the Central Office.
   B. Applications
      1. All groups shall submit applications for use of a school building or grounds to the Principal of the school on forms provided for that purpose. Applications for the use of school buildings or grounds must be completed and submitted to the school at least one week prior to the date of requested use.
      2. Groups holding regular meetings throughout the year need file only one application at the beginning of each school year.

However, special events by such groups must be covered by separate applications whenever they occur.

3. Approved applications shall be issued by the Principal on the prescribed form, and routed as follows:
   a. Original to the group or organization
   b. Green copy to Director of Operations
   c. Pink copy to Director of Public Safety, County Building, Montgomery County, Maryland
   d. Blue copy to Custodian
   e. Yellow copy to be filed at school.
4. The permission extended to any group to use the buildings or grounds of the public schools of Montgomery County shall expire automatically at the end of the fiscal year in which such permission is granted.

C. Reimbursement
   1. The Board of Education shall be reimbursed via the schools for certain expenses which it incurs as the result of outside organizations using the schools. All Type A organizations shall reimburse the Board via the schools for its additional salary expenses for custodial and cafeteria employees. In addition, all Type A groups (except Volunteer Fire Departments, school sponsored organizations, and approved hospitals of the County), shall reimburse the Board via the schools in the event that they use kitchen facilities. This reimbursement shall accompany the application and be submitted to the Principal. Groups submitting applications for regular meetings throughout the year shall arrange to make reimbursement in advance of each future meeting, or they may make payment in one check in advance for the full year. The following schedule of reimbursements shall prevail for all custodial overtime caused by the presence of class A groups (custodial overtime is that time which a custodian must spend in the school beyond his regular work schedule — the Principal shall determine what custodial overtime is required due to the use of his building by class A groups) — if the custodian has to come back to the school from his home to open the school for a group, the custodian's overtime shall be computed portal to portal, but travel time shall not exceed one-half hour each way:

a. For Custodian — $2.40 per hour (if overtime is necessary). The entire amount thus collected by the school shall be paid by the Board of Education (less necessary deductions) to the custodial personnel putting in the overtime. The following schedule of reimbursements shall prevail for the use of school kitchens, for Cafeteria Personnel:

(1) Managers — $4.00 per hour

(2) Workers — $2.40 per hour

The entire amount thus collected by the school shall be paid by the Board of Education (less necessary deductions) to the cafeteria personnel putting in the overtime.

b. For the kitchen — (for each 4 hours)

(1) Elementary School — $7.50

(2) Secondary School — $15.00

2. Checks and money orders must be made payable to the school being used. Do not make checks payable to individuals.

III. *Custodial Service*

A. The Principal of a school is responsible for its use and is required to be on duty at all times when a school building is in use unless he designates one of the following persons to be on duty: Custodian, Vice Principal, Trustee.

B. Principals may request the services of additional custodians in proportion to the size of the group or groups to be accommodated or activities thereof.

C. Custodial services shall include unlocking and locking the building, operation of lights, heating the building, setting up chairs, normal clean-up and putting the room(s) in order for their regular use.

IV. *Responsibility*

A. Any group of persons using a public school building is responsible for any damage above normal wear and tear, and is expected to:

1. Make necessary arrangements so that a representative of the applying group, acceptable to the principal, will be present during the time the building is being used.

2. Assign one person to direct, and to be responsible for the use of the building.

3. Locate the school's representative upon entering the building, and with him insure that:
   a. Exit doors are unlocked and free from obstruction in the area being used;
   b. Exit lights are turned on;
   c. Locations of fire extinguishers are known;
   d. Fire and police regulations are observed.
B. Groups of persons using a school building may be held responsible for suits brought by persons who have sustained bodily injury as a result of their attendance at non-public school sponsored functions.
C. Continued use of a school building by any group is contingent upon the group's taking proper steps to protect the school property and to insure complete safety, the observance of the prohibition against smoking in public school buildings (except in areas posted otherwise), and the reimbursement to the Board of Education of its expenses. If any Principal feels that his building is being misused by any groups, it is the duty of the Principal to point out the misuse to the group so that, through the cooperation of the group, the misuses may be stopped. If continued misuses occur, the Principal shall report this to the Director of Operations who shall (in cooperation with the appropriate Department Head if educational matters are involved) investigate the complaint and determine if the group should be prohibited from any further use of the county schools.

V. *General*

A. Responsibility for the building and grounds rests with the Principal at all times.
B. Any group or organization using school property shall save the County, the School Board, the individual members thereof, and any school officials or employees (free and without harm) from any loss, damage liability or expense that may arise during, or be caused in any way by such use or occupancy of school property.
C. Evening use of a school building must be terminated by midnight. There shall be no morning use (use before the regular day) on school days unless such activity is sponsored by school or PTA. No use of school buildings by outside groups shall

be permitted which would conflict time-wise with the regular school day schedule with the exception of use by the Board of Supervisors of Elections.

D. Cafeteria equipment shall be used only with the specific approval of the Principal and the Cafeteria Manager in consultation with the Supervisor of School Lunch.

E. If the all-purpose room in a school is being used as a classroom on an everyday basis it shall normally be available for use only to school and PTA groups.

F. Any church or church group shall be permitted to use schools in the County for a period of as much as three years (either consecutively or cumulatively) and any extension beyond three years will be limited to one year upon the approval of the Superintendent of Schools.

G. Groups using the schools on a repetitive basis will be allowed to store materials in the school, provided that such storage does not interfere with the school program. This will be determined by the Principal.

H. If an application is received from any group which does not fall in a category on the List of Organizations or Type of Organizations Authorized To Use the Public Schools of Montgomery County, Maryland, the Principal shall forward the application to the Operations Department, which department shall decide upon the eligibility of the group to use the schools.

I. If any Principal is going to deny the use of his school to any group which is authorized to use the public schools of Montgomery County for any reason other than the two listed immediately below, he shall first have to get the concurrence of the Director of Operations. If the Director of Operations does not concur in the denial, the group shall be permitted to use the school. Reasons sufficient for the Principal to deny the application of an approved group without referral to the Director of Operations are as follows:

1. The space applied for has already been committed to another group.

2. The space applied for may not be used for the purpose requested under these regulations.

List of the Organizations or Type of Organizations
Authorized to Use the Public Schools of
Montgomery County, Maryland

Type A Groups

The following organizations are required to pay for custodial overtime:

1. Recognized charitable or welfare groups
2. Religious organizations
3. Non-profit groups sponsoring educational or cultural programs for persons of more than high school age.*
4. Educational programs for persons of high school age or under (such as dancing classes, music classes, baton classes, gym classes, etc.)* These activities must be sponsored by one of the following (or by the PTA's, but if sponsored by the PTA's, the Board of Education will pay the custodial overtime) :**
   a. The Montgomery County Rec. Dept. (Any fees to be collected by the Board from the Montgomery County Rec. Dept. shall be collected by the Board and not by the individual schools)
   b. Old Georgetown Arts Group
   c. Community Arts Assoc.
   d. Recognized Cooperative Nursery Schools
5. Organized public recreation departments where available for all adult recreation programs except for such activities sponsored by PTA's or PTA Councils.
6. Adult theatrical groups if organized on a non-profit basis.
7. Civic organizations
8. Political organizations or groups of citizens interested in holding meetings to discuss political issues or candidates, provided such meetings are in accord with "the public interest," as interpreted under Limitations of Use.

* If any fee or tuition is charged for attendance, the teachers and the instructional programs must both be approved by the State Dept. of Ed. before the program may begin. Forms for applying to the State Dept. for approval may be obtained from the Director of Operations.

** See "Supplemental Instructions Governing After School Instructional Programs Conducted by Non-Public School Groups"

9. Recreational activities for and by County children (of a high school age and under) when sponsored by recognized, non-profit organizations such as local church groups, scouts, brownies, YMCA, YWCA, etc.
10. Montgomery Symphony and Adventure Theatre
11. Public school sponsored children's activities for which a charge is made.
12. Volunteer Fire Departments*
13. Approved hospitals of the County*
14. Montgomery County Recreation Department
15. Reserve Training organizations
16. Meetings of town governments

* These groups do not have to reimburse the Board of Education for the use of the school kitchens.

Type B Groups

Any necessary overtime brought about through the use of the schools by the following groups will be at no expense to the groups. If custodial overtime will be required as a result of the use of the schools by these groups, the schools must contact the Director of Operations before the event takes place so that the best method for handling the extra work may be arranged.

1. Board of Education meetings and activities; child study groups.
2. School sponsored activities (if no admission charges).
3. MCEA meetings.
4. Use by the County Council and departments (other than Recreation) of the County Government.
5. N.I.H. (Public Health Programs).
6. Elections under aegis of County Board of Election Supervisors.
7. Use for Civil Defense meetings if meeting is organized by and space is applied for by the Montgomery County Civil Defense Agency.
8. All meetings and activities of PTA's and PTA Councils.

SUPPLEMENTAL INSTRUCTIONS GOVERNING AFTER-SCHOOL
INSTRUCTIONAL PROGRAMS CONDUCTED BY NON-PUBLIC
SCHOOL GROUPS FOR SCHOOL AGE CHILDREN

The Board of Education approves the use of school buildings for after-school recreational and creative activities, such as: Children's dance, music, drama classes, etc., provided that:

1. Such activities in no way interfere with the regular school program, and the teacher's normal after-school routines. This shall be determined by the principal of each school.
2. Classroom organization and instructional materials are left after the activity as they were placed by the classroom teacher.
3. Such activities are conducted in a manner consistent with sound educational principles, so that school and community programs will be mutually supplementary.
4. Teachers participating in the programs are certified by the State Department of Education, and the programs are approved by the State Department of Education.
5. These classes have no organizational or contractual relations with a non-public school agency, and each teacher is employed on an individual basis and not as director of or teacher at a private school.
6. Such activities are sponsored by the organizations set forth in the Regulations for the Use of School Buildings and Grounds, which organizations are willing to assume responsibility for the necessary financial and administrative details, and which can provide evidence of a community interest and desire for the proposed program, and thus insure that no school is used as a private studio.
7. Regardless of sponsorship, no advertising of programs or class schedules be used which mentions the name of a studio or other commercial organization.
8. These programs are developed as extra-curricular activities to benefit the children, and not primarily as fund-raising projects for any groups. Charges should be based primarily on the costs of the program, such as teacher fee, custodial fee, and materials.
9. That the sponsoring organization is responsible financially for any breakage or excessive use of equipment.
10. When the P.T.A.'s are the sponsors, they shall assume responsibility for seeing:

a. That the programs offered are agreed upon by a vote of the membership.
b. That the programs are planned in coordination with the principal and supervised by the P.T.A.
c. That the programs are open primarily to children in the sponsoring school, and to children of other schools, at the discretion of the principal and P.T.A. of the school.
d. That all moneys and financial transactions are handled by the P.T.A.
e. That all administrative details are cared for by the P.T.A. with the advice and supervision of the principal.

BETHLEHEM JOINT SCHOOLS
FREDERICKTOWN, PENNSYLVANIA
[furnished by Dr. J. Vincen Connolley, Supervising Principal]

GENERAL REGULATIONS FOR USE OF BETHLEHEM JOINT SCHOOLS
BUILDINGS AND/OR FACILITIES FOR ACTIVITIES NOT INCLUDED
IN THE EDUCATIONAL PROGRAM OF THE SCHOOL SYSTEM

1. *Availability*

   All applications for facilities are dependent upon the availability of the facilities. The School and its organizations have prior right to use all facilities.

2. *Limits*

   The use of the facilities of Bethlehem Joint Schools shall be restricted to organizations within the School Area, and to organizations within the School Area acting as hosts to Area or District Meetings of their organization.

   No facility of the school system shall be let or donated to any organization for Sunday use.

3. *Applications*

   All applications for the use of the facilities of the Bethlehem Joint Schools shall be made to the office of the Supervising Principal on a form prepared for this purpose. Such applications must be made in time to permit their being reviewed by the Board of School Directors or a committee of the Board.

4. *Approval*

   All applications are subject to the approval of the School Administration and/or a committee of the Board and/or the Board of School Directors as conditions may demand.

5. *Concession*

   The Board of School Directors reserves the right for the Student Council or other school organization to operate the check room and the refreshment stands for their profit and the user agrees to operate no concession on the School property without the consent of the administration and/or a committee of the Board and/or the Board of School Directors.

6. *Damages*

   Thefts

   The applicant and/or the organization shall be responsible for all thefts of school property and/or damage thereto and shall reimburse the school district for such thefts or damage. All damages shall be based on the replacement costs.

7. *Police*

School Officials have the responsibility to engage Police for duty at the event and the applicant and/or the organization will be charged at the prevailing rate for their services. School employees on duty during the period of rental may call the police when, in their judgement, it becomes necessary.

8. *Admission*

The organization requesting the use of the school facilities shall have control of those who may be admitted to the activity, except that School Board members, school officials, and designated employees shall not be refused admission for administrative, supervisory or custodial purposes.

9. *Equipment*

All apparatus, equipment, and devices owned by the school shall be operated by school employees at the expense of the organization.

10. *Decorations*

(a) All decorations used within the buildings must be fireproof as possible and are subject to the approval of the school officials. No open flame decorations shall be permitted, and no decorations shall be fastened to the walls or ceiling with nails, screws, scotch tape, or other fastener that will damage the finish of the wall.

(b) Decorations in the auditorium, cafeteria, gymnasium, or foyer shall be limited to floral and flag decorations or those of a free standing informative display type.

11. *Clean-up*

(a) All decorations, furnishings, and equipment provided by the rentor shall be installed and debris removed by the user under the direction and supervision of the school staff. Debris must be removed before the facilities are again needed for school purposes.

(b) There shall be no installations of equipment or alterations to existing facilities or equipment by the user without approval of school officials.

12. *Smoking*

Smoking will not be permitted in any part of a building except in the cafeteria dining room in connection with a dinner meeting.

13. *Drinking*

Intoxicants shall not be permitted on the premises.

14. *Gambling*

Gambling is prohibited in any building or on any premises.

15. *Bond*

Insurance

The applicant and/or the organization agrees to assume all responsibility for damage or liability of any kind and further agrees to save harmless the school system from any expense or costs in connection with the use of the school facilities under this agreement. The Board of School Directors may require the applicant and/or the organization to furnish a Bond and/or a Certificate of Insurance to guarantee the conditions of this agreement or any liability incurred by it.

16. *Right to Refuse*

The School Board reserves the right to refuse the use of its buildings and grounds to any organization for reason.

17. *Payments*

All operating costs incurred by this agreement with the Board of School Directors shall be paid to the Board within ten (10) days prior to date of event, and all debts or other costs shall be paid within ten (10) days after the date of the event. All employees of the school system or school-connected personnel will be paid by the Board or its agencies. Checks are payable to the "Treasurer, Bethlehem Joint Schools."

18. *Emergency*

In the event of a local, state, or national emergency, disaster or preparation for same, appropriate facilities of the School System will be made available to those affected.

19. *Contract*

After the application has been approved and signed by school authorities and representatives of the organization, it becomes a contract with the applicant and/or the organization, and they may not sublet or transfer their rights or privileges to any individual, group, or organization.

POLICY FOR RENTING SCHOOL FACILITIES
(REQUESTS FALL IN THREE CLASSES)

Class I

All groups or organizations working directly or indirectly for the interest of the students: (P.T.A.'s, Band Mothers, Alumnae, Workshops, etc.)
Senior and Junior High...No rental fee.

Class II

Civic organizations, service organizations and religious organizations who request the use of the school facilities for a business meeting or for raising money for themselves or other projects.

SENIOR HIGH
Fee for meetings only.

    a. Classroom — regular size — to be designated by the Supervising Principal
    $5.00 .... Fee
    b. Cafeteria —
        $10.00 — without kitchen facilities.
        $20.00 — with kitchen facilities, plus kitchen supervisor,
            plus our labor, plus menu if we supply.
    c. Auditorium — $50.00 .... Fee

JUNIOR HIGH — whether used as gymnasium or auditorium.
    Meetings only — $15.00
    Profit making — $15.00 plus 20% of gross receipts.

Class III
SENIOR HIGH

All other persons, groups or organizations such as political, fraternal or any individual.

    a. Room .... not available
    b. Cafeteria .... not available
    c. Gymnasium .... not available
    d. Auditorium
        $100.00 — Meeting only.
        Profit making — $100.00 plus 50% of gross receipts.

JUNIOR HIGH
    Meetings only — $25.00
    Profit making — $25.00 plus 20% of gross receipts.

KALISPELL SCHOOL DISTRICT
KALISPELL, MONTANA
[furnished by Mr. D. P. Langbell, Superintendent]

PART "G" — OUT-OF-SCHOOL GROUP USE OF SCHOOL FACILITIES

Following are the rules and the schedule of the use of the school areas of the Kalispell Elementary Schools. The rule and schedule are effective as of January 8, 1952 by order of the Trustees of School District No. 5, Kalispell, Montana.

Philosophy:

A middle ground had to be taken between two philosophies on use of school building facilities by out-of-public school groups. One is that the buildings are for the specific use of the children of school age. The other is that the schools are built and supported by the groups within the community, therefore are entitled to the use of the buildings at any time. A middle ground is that the schools are to be given first to the use of school groups and that available time may be used by out-of-school groups. Since the groups do not include all of the community, it shall be reasonable to charge a fee for use which will pay for custodial help plus administrative costs. No attempt is made to charge for cost of heating and lighting, as this would be prohibitive.

Regulations:

1. Arrangements for the use of any building must be made in advance with the Superintendent of Schools.
2. Guarantee for rent in form of a deposit may be required.
3. No one but a janitor, principal or teacher may allow admittance to any building. Keys are not to be given to a representative of any group using the area.
4. The custodian or his substitute is to lock building after use.
5. No smoking in any part of the building.
6. Alcohol or any alcoholic beverage is not to be allowed in the building.
7. Each group is to use its own equipment, not that of the school unless special arrangements are made in advance. Under no condition shall materials or equipment be taken from student lockers or baskets.

8. Each group is responsible to see that only its members are admitted.
9. In programs and contests where public is present, the group shall be held responsible for conduct and any damage resulting.
10. Rental fee is due at the School Office in the Central Building within 24 hours after use.
11. Political and religious groups must obtain special Board of Trustee permission to use facilities.
12. Proper and accepted foot-wear shall be used by any group to insure care of the floors. (Hob-nailed shoes and/or soles causing marks not to be used on floors.)
13. Facilities are not for rental or use on Sundays.
14. Use of the kitchen in any school may be made with additional charge of one (1) dollar, provided premises and utensils are left clean.
15. Payments to custodians or substitutes are to be made by the school.
16. Any violation of any of the preceding regulations will remove group from further use of facilities.

Rental Fees:

The rental charge to all out-of-public school groups shall be: Five dollars ($5.00) per hour with a minimum of ten dollars ($10.00).

Custodian Pay:

1. For opening and closing buildings . . . . $ 1.00
2. For need to clean when building is used less than one and one-half hour . . . . $ 1.50
3. For supervision and cleaning for session of more than one and one-half hour up to three hours $10.00
4. For item No. 3 over three hours . . . . $ 5.00

I, ..., a representative

of the group known as the ....,

which desires to use the .... in ....

building, on the follow day or dates : ....
have read the above regulations and rates and do hereby promise
conformity.

Signed : ....

Date : ....

No charge for school group use, other than janitor costs which
average $1.50 per hour.

WILLOUGHBY-EASTLAKE CITY SCHOOL DISTRICT
WILLOUGHBY, OHIO
[furnished by Dr. Guy F. Eberhart, Superintendent]

WILLOUGHBY-EASTLAKE CITY SCHOOL DISTRICT
4284 Center Street
Willoughby, Ohio

APPLICATION FOR USE OF PUBLIC SCHOOL BUILDINGS

(APPLICANTS WILL PLEASE FURNISH THE FOLLOWING INFORMATION IN QUADRUPLICATE.)
(Please Print)

Date of Application_____,19____

_____ _____ _____
NAME OF ORGANIZATION   ADDRESS   PHONE

_____ _____ _____
NAME AND TITLE OF INDIVIDUAL   ADDRESS   PHONE

_____
TYPE OF PROGRAM OR EVENT

Estimate of number of persons expected to attend_____ Amount of Admission Fee $_____ Is Collection to be taken?_____

For what purpose is Fee or Collection to be used?_____

Name of School to be used _____ Room or part of Building desired _____

_____Date or Dates on which Building is to be used_____

Hours of Day or Night_____ Number of Folding Chairs required_____ Will your organization

require use of any equipment or re-arrangement of room?_____ If so, please give information here_____

_____ Services required other than of caretaker attendant_____

_____ Will refreshments or lunch be served?_____ Nature of lunch _____

_____ Name of person or persons to be in authority _____

_____

If said permission is granted, we hereby agree to comply strictly with the rules and regulations of the Board of Education governing the use of public school buildings as set forth on the back of the original application.

(Signed)_____ _____
                   SIGNATURE   TITLE

- -

PERMIT FOR USE OF SCHOOL BUILDINGS

Date_____, 19_____

You have been granted the use of_____ School for the purpose of_____.

_____ on _____ between the hours of_____and_____

in accordance with the conditions as signed by you on the above application.

FEE $_____ All payments to be made in advance. Other remarks_____

_____

(Signed)_____ _____
                   SIGNATURE   TITLE
SCHOOL PRINCIPAL

Community Use of School Facilities

One of the primary responsibilities of the Board of Education is to provide school buildings and facilities for children of school age in this community and to permit full and extended use of this group. The Board also recognizes that these facilities are, to a large degree, financed and supported by the citizens of the community and, therefore, these facilities should be made available for community use. Thus, it shall be the general policy of this Board of Education that all school facilities shall be first made available for the school program and community use of these facilities will be encouraged in so far as such use does not interfere with school activities.

The Board of Education has the responsibility for protecting all school facilities against damage and from increased operating costs due to extended and after school use of such facilities. Certain rules and regulations pertaining to such use must be adopted and certain fees must be charged to cover the additional operating expenses incurred.

The following regulations and fees are intended to accomplish the purpose of permitting and encouraging full use of school facilities to the general public without decreasing the use of such facilities to the school itself. These regulations and fees are of a general nature and each building Principal may adopt such specific rules as may be necessary to control the use of specific areas or facilities in each building.

Building Regulations

1. All applications for the use of school premises shall be submitted to the building Principal. During vacation periods when the building Principal is not on duty, applications should be submitted to the Business Office.
2. The persons or group receiving the permit shall be responsible in case of loss or damage, if any, to school property including that belonging to students or school employees.
3. The school shall have first claim to the use of the building at all times, and any agreement made with an organization must be contingent on the needs of the program of the school, and such agreement may be terminated or altered at any time.

4. All meetings by any group or organization shall be non-exclusive and shall be open to the general public.

5. Requests for the use of buildings must be made not less than forty-eight (48) hours before the date on which the facilities are to be used; the cancellation requests must be not less than twenty-four (24) hours in advance. Permit holders will be held responsible for all charges if cancellation notice is not received twenty-four (24) hours in advance.

6. Permits will not be granted for the personal or individual use of school property and equipment except when a written request is submitted to the Board of Education and formal approval is authorized by the Board.

7. All permits will be issued for specific rooms in school buildings and it shall be the responsibility of the organization to see that the remainder of the building is not entered or molested. The organization must provide competent adult supervision for all activities.

8. When school cafeterias are used, the school cafeteria supervisor, or other designated school employee, must be present and have general supervision of school equipment. The fee for this service must be paid by the organization using cafeteria facilities according to established rates. Arrangements for the use of cafeterias must be made with the manager of all school cafeterias at the Business Office.

9. There shall be no smoking in the school buildings except in those rooms provided for this purpose and designated by the school principal. Alcoholic beverages or liquors shall not be permitted on school property at any time.

10. Any right or privilege granted to any person, persons, or organizations to use any building or property is personal and shall not be transferred to any other person, persons, or organizations.

11. The permit holder agrees to save and hold harmless the Willoughby-Eastlake City School District and agrees to assume responsibility for all liabilities arising incident to the occupancy of building use, it being understood and agreed that the public schools assume no obligation respecting the use of such premises.

12. Any decorations shall be erected in a manner that will not be destructive to school property, and such erection shall be approved by the custodian on duty. All decorations shall be removed from the building before eight o'clock A.M. on the next day after the

building has been used. The use of any materials on floors or other parts of the building without specific approval of the custodian on duty is strictly prohibited.

13. The permit holder will assume responsibility for securing police protection when it is deemed that such police attendance is necessary.

14. Buildings will be open one-half hour before the scheduled time of the program and closed one-quarter hour after the scheduled end of the program. Any extrà time will be charged for at the regular rate in multiples of one-half hour.

15. Charges will be determined and are payable at least twenty-four (24) hours in advance of the date reserved to the office of the school principal who will forward the funds to the Business Office of the Board of Education.

16. All advertising except that incidental to programs, and all sale of merchandise, printed matter, or other material is forbidden unless special approval is given by the Superintendent of Schools.

17. The use of the school building on regular school days shall be permitted during the following hours only: Afternoons from four (4) until six (6) o'clock. Evenings from seven (7) until twelve (12) o'clock. On Saturdays, Sundays, and holidays, no school building or any room or rooms therein shall be opened for any purpose other than necessary cleaning, except upon written application and approval on the required building use form. In no case will any building be open for use after 12:00 P.M.

18. School equipment such as projectors and public address systems and stage equipment may not be used by outside organizations without the service of school operators. If such equipment is desired, special arrangements must be made with the Principal of the school concerned. No other special or extra equipment is included in the permit. Physical education, science, business, or any other equipment or supplies will not be used by any group except school organizations.

FEE SCHEDULE FOR USE OF BUILDINGS, GROUNDS, OR EQUIPMENT

Class I

No fee shall be charged for the use of buildings, equipment, and grounds by school organizations, P.T.A. groups, athletic and band booster groups. The school Principal will be required to control the free use of buildings by these organizations. These groups must be responsible for special room or equipment arrangements that may be required. The custodian in charge will give reasonable supervisory assistance but cannot be expected to assist to the detriment of his regular scheduled work. For example each school club will be responsible for any furniture arrangement that may be necessary in order to hold a special activity such as a dance.

A fee of $2.75 per hour shall be charged to all groups for the use of kitchen facilities on weekdays or $4.00 per hour when used on Saturdays, Sundays, or holidays. This fee for the use of the school kitchen shall include the service of one cafeteria worker. For each additional worker that may be required, a fee of $2.00 per hour shall be charged for weekday service and $3.00 per hour shall be charged for Saturday, Sunday, or holiday service. An additional charge of $2.00 per hour shall be charged for P.T.A. and Booster profit-making ventures for kitchen utility charges.

When P.T.A. groups and Booster groups use school buildings for profit-making ventures, an additional fee of $1.50 per hour shall be charged for light and if required, a fee of $2.00 per hour shall be charged for heat. A fee of $3.00 per hour shall be charged for each custodian or maintenance worker that may be required.

Class II

No fee shall be charged for the use of school facilities by such organizations as Boy Scouts, Girl Scouts, Cub Scouts, Blue Birds, Y.M.C.A. organizations, municipal recreational committees, civic, political, and other allied organizations when buildings are attended by school custodians in the performance of their regular duties. When buildings are required to be opened on a Saturday or Sunday or at other times when a regular attendant is not on duty or when additional services are required for setting up and cleaning areas by the regular custodian crew, a fee of $3.00 per hour shall be charged for the labor service of each attendant.

A fee of $3.00 per hour shall be charged to these groups for the use of kitchen facilities on weekdays and $4.50 per hour on Saturdays, Sundays, or holidays. For each additional cafeteria worker that may be required, a fee of $2.00 per hour shall be charged for weekday service and $3.00 per hour for weekend or holiday service. An additional $2.50 per hour shall be charged for profit-making ventures to cover utility costs.

When these groups use school facilities for profit-making ventures, an additional fee of $1.50 per hour shall be charged for light and if required, a fee of $2.00 per hour shall be charged for heat.

Class III

Class III fees shall be charged for the use of school facilities by religious, charitable, philanthropic, service clubs, fine arts associations, theatre groups, independent recreational groups, and other organizations not operating for profit and devoted to community interest and child welfare. Class III-A shall be used for groups using school facilities such as auditoriums for practice purposes and when the total number of persons using the facility is less than twenty-five individuals, the fees for Class III are listed on the attached schedule.

Class IV

This fee shall be charged for use of school facilities by organized groups within the community for profit and when such profit is used by group for the advancement of the group. These fees are listed on the attached schedule.

Class V

This fee shall be charged for school facilities used by groups *not* within the community for non-profit, religious, charitable, philanthropic, civic, or other non-commercial, non-personal purposes. Fees for Class V are listed on the attached schedule.

Class VI

Class VI fees shall be charged for the use of school facilities by groups *not* within the community for profit purposes and when such profit is used by the group for advancement of the group. These fees are listed on the attached schedule.

Other Fees and Considerations

An additional fee of four dollars ($4.00) per hour shall be charged for the use of the Public Address System and a total fee of four dollars ($4.00) for the use of a projector and screen or for the use of other stage equipment by Class III, IV, V, and VI permit holders. The above charges include the service of operators. The fee as charged for the use of school kitchens includes the service of one cafeteria worker. An additional two dollars ($2.00) per hour shall be charged for each additional worker for weekdays and three dollars ($3.00) per hour for weekend use. The fees for buildings as listed include the service of one caretaker attendant. If the service of more than one person is required, the fee shall be increased three dollars ($3.00) per hour for each additional person.

The hourly rate that is applied shall begin at the time the building is opened for the group or any part of the group. Normally this charge would start one-half hour before the scheduled time of the program. The rate shall end when the building is closed which would normally be one-quarter hour after the scheduled end of the program.

The fee schedule for Class III, IV, V, and VI permit holders lists the charges for one particular area in a building. When a request is made for more than one area, the charge for the secondary area shall be one-half the fee as set forth in the fee schedule. The fees listed for kitchen or athletic field use shall be charged regardless of the number of other areas requested.

Unusual requests not covered by regulations or fees as listed will be considered as irregular permits and may be submitted to the Business Office of the Board of Education for consideration.

Fee Schedule

Class	Weekday During Regular School Term		Saturday, Sunday, Holiday, Vacation Period		Add for Use During Oct. 15-Apr. 15	Add for Shower Room If Used	Add for Deprec.
Elementary School Gym or Playroom:							
III	1 hr. 4.00,	Add. hr. 1.00	1 hr. 6.70,	Add. hr. 3.70	Ea. hr. 1.90	2.80	-0-
III-A	" " 1.25	" " 1.00	" " 4.00	" " 3.70	" " 1.90	2.80	-0-
IV	" " 10.00	" " 2.00	" " 13.00	" " 4.00	" " 2.00	5.00	2.00
V	" " 10.00	" " 1.00	" " 12.70	" " 3.70	" " 1.90	4.60	2.00
VI	" " 10.00	" " 2.00	" " 13.00	" " 4.00	" " 2.00	5.00	5.00
Secondary School Gym:							
III	1 hr. 17.80,	Add. hr. 1.50	1 hr. 20.50,	Add. hr. 4.20	Ea. hr. 1.90	3.75	-0-
III-A	" " 6.20	" " 1.50	" " 8.90	" " 4.20	" " 1.90	3.75	-0-
IV	" " 25.75	" " 3.00	" " 26.00	" " 5.00	" " 2.00	5.00	12.25
V	" " 25.75	" " 1.50	" " 24.00	" " 4.25	" " 1.90	4.00	12.25
VI	" " 25.75	" " 3.00	" " 26.00	" " 5.00	" " 2.00	5.00	25.00

Class	Weekday During Regular School Term			Saturday, Sunday, Holiday, Vacation Period			Add for Use During Oct. 15-Apr. 15	Add for Shower Room If Used	Add for Deprec.

Auditoriums:

Class									
III	1 hr. 6.15,	Add. hr.	1.00	1 hr. 8.45,	Add. hr.	3.70	Ea. hr. 2.25	-0-	-0-
III-A	" " 1.25	" "	1.00	" " 5.95	" "	3.70	" " 2.25	-0-	-0-
IV	" " 19.15	" "	2.00	" " 22.00	" "	5.00	" " 2.25	-0-	5.00
V	" " 19.15	" "	1.00	" " 20.20	" "	3.70	" " 2.25	-0-	5.00
VI	" " 19.15	" "	3.00	" " 22.00	" "	5.00	" " 2.25	-0-	10.00

Classroom:

Class									
III	1 hr. 2.65,	Add. hr.	.25	1 hr. 2.67,	Add. hr.	1.50	Ea. hr. .50	-0-	-0-
IV	" " 3.60	" "	.50	" " 7.00	" "	3.00	" " 1.00	-0-	.50
V	" " 3.60	" "	.25	" " 6.30	" "	2.95	" " .50	-0-	.50
VI	" " 3.60	" "	1.00	" " 7.00	" "	3.50	" " 2.00	-0-	1.00

Cafeteria: (Lunch Room)

Class									
III	1 hr. 27.25,	Add. hr.	1.20	1 hr. 29.95,	Add. hr.	3.90	Ea. hr. 1.50	-0-	-0-
IV	" " 33.25	" "	1.50	" " 36.50	" "	4.00	" " 2.00	-0-	5.50
V	" " 33.25	" "	1.20	" " 35.95	" "	3.90	" " 1.50	-0-	5.50
VI	" " 33.25	" "	2.00	" " 36.50	" "	4.50	" " 3.00	-0-	10.00

Social Area:

Class									
III	1 hr. 10.30,	Add. hr.	2.75	1 hr. 13.00,	Add. hr.	5.45	Ea. hr. 1.50	-0-	-0-
IV	" " 15.70	" "	3.00	" " 19.00	" "	6.00	" " 1.75	-0-	6.00
V	" " 15.70	" "	2.75	" " 18.40	" "	5.45	" " 1.50	-0-	6.00
VI	" " 15.70	" "	3.50	" " 19.00	" "	6.50	" " 2.00	-0-	12.00

Athletic Field:

Class									
III	1 hr. 30.00,	Add. hr.	5.50	1 hr. 32.50,	Add. hr.	10.00	-0-	14.00	-0-
IV	" " 30.00	" "	6.00	" " 35.00	" "	12.00	-0-	16.00	20.00
V	" " 39.00	" "	5.50	" " 32.50	" "	10.00	-0-	14.00	20.00
VI	" " 30.00	" "	10.00	" " 35.00	" "	12.00	-0-	16.00	40.00

School Playground:

Class									
III	1 hr. 2.25,	Add. hr.	1.00	1 hr. 4.95,	Add. hr.	3.70	-0-	10.00	-0-
IV	" " 5.00	" "	2.00	" " 7.00	" "	4.00	-0-	16.00	5.00
V	" " 3.00	" "	1.00	" " 6.00	" "	3.70	-0-	14.00	5.00
VI	" " 5.00	" "	2.00	" " 7.00	" "	4.00	-0-	16.00	10.00

Elementary or Secondary School Kitchen or Snack Bar or Concession Stand: (Limited Use)

Class									
III	1 hr. 4.00,	Add. hr.	2.75	1 hr. 5.25,	Add. hr.	4.00	-0-	-0-	-0-
IV	" " 5.00	" "	3.00	" " 6.00	" "	4.00	-0-	-0-	2.00
V	" " 5.00	" "	2.75	" " 5.25	" "	4.00	-0-	-0-	2.00
VI	" " 5.00	" "	3.00	" " 6.50	" "	4.00	-0-	-0-	4.00

Elementary School Kitchen: (General Use)

Class									
III	1 hr. 6.00,	Add. hr.	2.75	1 hr. 6.25,	Add. hr.	4.25	-0-	-0-	-0-
IV	" " 7.00	" "	3.00	" " 8.00	" "	5.00	-0-	-0-	4.00
V	" " 6.00	" "	2.75	" " 6.25	" "	4.25	-0-	-0-	4.00
VI	" " 7.00	" "	3.00	" " 8.00	" "	5.00	-0-	-0-	8.00

Secondary School Kitchen: (General Use)

Class									
III	1 hr. 8.00,	Add. hr.	2.75	1 hr. 9.00,	Add. hr.	5.00	-0-	-0-	-0-
IV	" " 10.00	" "	3.00	" " 11.00	" "	6.00	-0-	-0-	8.00
V	" " 8.00	" "	2.75	" " 9.00	" "	5.00	-0-	-0-	8.00
VI	" " 10.00	" "	3.00	" " 11.00	" "	6.00	-0-	-0-	16.00

GLOSSARY

Action — An ordinary proceeding in a court by which one party prosecutes another for the enforcement or protection of a right, the redress of a wrong, or the punishment of a public offense. In common language, a suit or lawsuit.

Allegation — Statement in pleadings, setting forth what the party expects to prove.

Allege — To state, assert, or charge; to make an allegation.

Appellant — The party who takes an appeal from one court to another.

Arbitrary — Not supported by fair cause and without reason given.

Charter — A grant made by the sovereign either to the whole people or to a portion of them, securing to them the enjoyment of certain rights.

Citations — References to law books. A citation includes the book where the reference is found, the volume number, and section or page number. (See *Judicial citations.*)

Civil action — One brought to recover some civil right, or to obtain redress for some wrong.

Code — A compilation of statutes, scientifically arranged into chapters, subheadings, and sections, with a table of contents and index.

Common law — As here used, legal principles derived from usage and custom, or from court decisions affirming such usages and customs.

Concurring opinion — An opinion written by a judge who agrees with the majority of the court as to the decision in a case, but has different reasons for arriving at that decision.

Author's comment: Many of the terms included in this Glossary are reproduced from a list distributed to graduate students in School Law, through the courtesy of the Educational Administration Program at the University of Pittsburgh.

Constitution — The supreme organic and fundamental law of a nation or state, establishing the character and conception of its government, forming the basic principles to which its internal life is to be conformed, organizing the government, regulating, distributing, and limiting the functions of its different departments, and prescribing the extent and manner of the exercise of sovereign powers.

Contract — A deliberate engagement between competent parties, upon a consideration, to do, or to abstain from doing, some act.

    a. *Express contract* — One of which the terms are openly uttered or declared at the time of making it, being stated in distinct or explicit language, either orally or in writing.

    b. *Implied contract* — One not created or evidenced by explicit agreement by the parties, but inferred by law, as a matter of reason and justice.

    c. *Parol contract* — All contracts which are not contracts of record. Though a contract may be wholly in writing, it is still a parol contract if it is not under seal.

Damages — Pecuniary compensation or indemnity which may be recovered in court by the person who has suffered loss or injury to his person, property, or rights through the unlawful act, omission, or negligence of another.

De facto — Actually; in fact; in deed. A term used to denote a thing actually done.

Defendant — The party against whom relief or recovery is sought in a court action.

Defense — That which is offered and alleged by the defendant as a reason in law or fact why the plaintiff should not recover.

Dissenting opinion — The opinion in which a judge announces his dissent from the conclusions held by the majority of the court.

Due process — The exercise of the powers of government in such a way as to protect individual rights.

Eminent domain — The power to take private property for public use, whether exercised by the sovereign directly, or by one to whom the sovereign power has been delegated for public purposes.

Enjoin — To require a person, by writ of injunction from a court of equity, to perform, or to abstain or desist from, some act.

Ex rel. — Abbreviation for ex relations, meaning on relation or information. Here it need be explained only as designating a type of court decision.

Fee simple — An absolute estate of inheritance; the largest estate and most extensive interest that can be enjoyed in land, being the entire property therein, and it confers an unlimited power of alienation.

Governmental immunity — A particular privilege of, pertaining to, or proceeding from government.

Injunction — A prohibitive writ issued by a court of equity forbidding the defendant to do some act he is threatening, or forbidding him to continue doing some act which is injurious to the plaintiff and cannot be adequately redressed by an action at law. (See *Temporary injunction.*)

Judicial citations — References to court decisions. Citations in the case materials in this book refer to official state reports and to the National Reporter System. The volume number precedes the abbreviation of the Reporter, and the page number follows it. In parentheses is the name of the state where the decision was rendered, and its date. A complete judicial citation includes all sources where the case may be found. (See *Citations.*)

Legislative intent — Where the legislature has enacted two or more statutes which from their wording appear to be inconsistent, or in conflict with the state or federal constitutions there is an ambiguity, the courts construing the statutes are permitted to look beyond their words as to the legislative purpose.

Liability — The state of being bound or obliged in law or justice to do, pay, or make good something; legal responsibility.

Limited mandate — A particular privilege of, pertaining to, or proceeding from government but which is restricted in duration, extent, or scope. (See *Mandate.*)

Majority opinion — The statement of reasons for the views of the majority of the members of the bench in a decision to which some of them disagree.

Mandamus — A writ to compel a public body or its officers to perform a duty.

Mandate — A command, order, or direction, written or oral, which court is authorized to give and person is bound to obey. (See *Limited mandate.*)

Mandatory — Compulsory, referring to a command for which disregard or disobedience is unlawful.

Municipality — The body of officers taken collectively, belonging to a city, appointed to manage its affairs and defend its interests.

Permissive — That which may be done.

Petition — Written application or prayer to the court for the redress of of a wrong or the grant of a privilege or license.

Plaintiff — Person who brings an action; one who sues by filing a complaint.

Prayer — The part of the petition in which petitioner requests the court to grant relief sought.

Precedent — A decision considered as furnishing an example or authority for an identical or similar case afterward arising on a similar question of law.

Regulations — Rules for management or government.

Relator — An informer; the person upon whose complaint or at whose insistence certain writs are issued such as an information or writ of quo warrant, and who is quasi the plaintiff in the proceeding.

Relief — The redress or assistance which a complainant seeks from the court, not properly applied to money damages.

Res adjudicata — A matter judicially decided.

Respondent — The defendant in an action; a party adverse to an appellant in an action which is appealed to a higher court.

Restrain — To prohibit from action; to enjoin.

Right — A power or privilege in one person against another.

Sovereign immunity — See *Governmental immunity*.

Statute — Act of the legislature.

Statutory — Created or defined by a statute; required by a statute.

Supra — Above; upon.

Temporary injunction — An injunction granted by the beginning of a suit to restrain the defendant from doing some act, the right to which is in dispute, and which may be discharged or made permanent according to the result of the case after the rights of the parties are determined. (See *Injunction*.)

Ultra vires — A term used to express the action of a corporation which is beyond the power conferred upon it by its charter, or by the statutes under which it was instituted.

Void — Ineffectual, having no legal force or binding effect; said of a contract, a defective instrument which can be cured by ratification by the one who could have avoided it.

Warrant — A class of municipal securities, in the nature of a bill of exchange drawn by an officer of a municipality upon the treasurer thereof.

Writ of mandamus — An order which issues from a court of superior jurisdiction, and is directed to a private or municipal corporation, or any of its officers, or to an inferior court commanding the performance of a particular act therein specified or directing the restoration of the complainant to rights or privileges of which he has been illegally deprived.